Praise for *Everything*

"*Everything Worthy of Observation* is a delight to read. Not only does one see State landmarks such as Niagara Falls through fresh eyes (a neatly foiled snake attack at the Falls is recounted) but one almost feels the dust of stage coach travel. The hazards of canal travel are made clear—the large number of low bridges on the Erie Canal required that canal boat passengers 'lie down flat on the Deck . . . or get down below' to avoid receiving severe blows and getting knocked down. No doubt the pleasure of reading this book is greatly enhanced by the scholarship of Paul G. Schneider Jr. His extensive research is evident in the wonderful notes he provides that furnish context for the reader. I highly recommend this book."

— Margaret Lynch-Brennan, author of
*The Irish Bridget: Irish Immigrant Women in
Domestic Service in America, 1840–1930*

"Carefully transcribed and meticulously edited, the travel journal of Canadian Alexander Stewart Scott provides a close-up view of life in upstate New York in 1826. A cultivated devotee of the theater and of books and reading, Scott records many details during his canal and lake voyage. He describes meeting many interesting people during his travel, which included transportation not only on canal boats but also by stagecoach and steamboat. Scott has left us with a fascinating depiction of New York State during a significant period in its history."

— Paul R. Huey, Retired Senior Scientist (Archaeology),
New York State Office of Parks,
Recreation & Historic Preservation

Everything Worthy of Observation

Everything Worthy of Observation

THE 1826 NEW YORK STATE TRAVEL JOURNAL OF ALEXANDER STEWART SCOTT

Edited by

PAUL G. SCHNEIDER JR.

excelsior editions

AN IMPRINT OF STATE UNIVERSITY OF NEW YORK PRESS

Cover art: "Erie Canal," 1831 watercolor on board by J. W. Hill.
Courtesy of the Union College Permanent Collection.

Published by State University of New York Press, Albany

Excelsior Editions is an imprint of State University of New York Press

For information, contact State University of New York Press, Albany, NY
www.sunypress.edu

Library of Congress Cataloging-in-Publication Data

Names: Scott, Alexander Stewart, 1805–1846, author. | Schneider, Paul G., Jr., 1945– editor, writer of introduction, writer of afterword.
Title: Everything worthy of observation : the 1826 New York State travel journal of Alexander Stewart Scott / edited with an introduction and afterword by Paul G. Schneider Jr.
Description: Albany : State University of New York Press, [2019] | Series: Excelsior editions | Includes bibliographical references and index.
Identifiers: LCCN 2018036281 | ISBN 9781438475158 (hardcover : alk. paper) | ISBN 9781438475165 (paperback : alk. paper) | ISBN 9781438475172 (ebook)
Subjects: LCSH: Scott, Alexander Stewart, 1805–1846—Travel—New York (State)—Diaries. | New York (State)—Description and travel.
Classification: LCC F123 .S43 2019 | DDC 917.4704—dc23
LC record available at https://lccn.loc.gov/2018036281

10 9 8 7 6 5 4 3 2 1

Contents

Illustrations

Figures

Maps

Foreword

Every day, librarians help people identify resources and access a wide variety of information. As ever more information is available digitally, it is easy to forget that there is much information that can only be found by reading unique handwritten sources like letters and diaries. The Manuscripts and Special Collections unit of the New York State Library is the repository of thousands of these manuscripts. One such resource is *The 1826* [New York State] *Travel Journal of Alexander Stewart Scott* (BD13145).

Paul Schneider's transcription has made the contents of Alexander Scott's journal accessible to even a casual reader. The journal documents a three-month trip Scott took in 1826 from his home in Quebec, Canada, south to Albany, then west to Buffalo on the Erie Canal, and back to Quebec.

Having recently spent a week traveling on the Erie Canal, I could relate to many of Scott's comments about that portion of his trip, but anyone who has traveled or visited family and friends in other locations will be able to relate to his experiences. I particularly appreciated one of the entries he made about the last leg of his trip in Canada: "a long passage this; and which is rendered the more dull by the want of Books or something else to help one to kill time: a small Library is a very desirable thing on board of these public Packets, in this respect we are far inferior to the Americans, who and even in their Canal Boats have generally got a pretty good collection of works of different natures for the use of the Passengers . . ."

It is extremely gratifying to those of us in the New York State Library when this happens.

—Kathi L. Stanley
Associate Librarian (retired)
Manuscripts and Special Collections
New York State Library

Acknowledgments

Many people contributed their expertise, support, and encouragement toward making this publication possible. Matthew DeLaMater eagerly shared his discovery of, and enthusiasm for, Scott's travel journal and urged its eventual publication. The task of transcribing the journal would have proven far more time-consuming and onerous without the continuing assistance of the New York State Library's Manuscripts and Special Collections staff, among whom Vicki Weiss, Paul Mercer (now retired), Victor DesRosiers, and Kathi Stanley (now retired) deserve my warmest gratitude. When the possible publication of the journal was first mentioned, Vicki and Kathi immediately supported the idea. Kathi, as the head of Manuscripts and Special Collections, helped secure the library's permission to proceed. My thanks to former State Librarian Bernard Margolis (now deceased), who agreed to its publication.

Mary Doehla gave unstintingly of her time, critically reviewing and contributing insightful suggestions and corrections through several early drafts of the manuscript. Her practical help, excitement, and encouragement were enormously beneficial. Vicki Weiss willingly volunteered to proofread and comment on all the later manuscript drafts. Her sharp eye and knowledge caught many embarrassing errors, and her comments immeasurably improved the final text. I simply cannot thank her enough for her remarkable perseverance and assistance. She deserves great credit for helping make the publication of Scott's travel journal possible. Margaret Lynch-Brennan translated some of Scott's French phrases, helping me make sense of his intended meaning. The anonymous readers who reviewed the original manuscript and offered their probing insights, suggestions, and corrections have helped immeasurably to improve the final publication. The editorial and production staff of State University of New York Press deserve my special gratitude for their commitment to publishing Scott's journal, their patience with my many questions and unavoidable setbacks, and their dedicated efforts toward making this volume a reality. My thanks are extended to all these people, along with the acknowledgment that any remaining errors are mine alone.

For more than a decade, Brad Utter has been and remains an invaluable colleague whose friendship is intellectually and personally rewarding. Brad's knack of dangling intriguing historical projects under my ever-curious nose has led me down many a fascinating research avenue. Without his warm and never-failing support, my decision to redirect a long career in the history museum field toward becoming an independent historian would have been more difficult and certainly less rewarding.

How is it that spouses typically are given credit only at the end of acknowledgments, when I'm guessing that, like mine, their names should appear first? Robin Campbell, a professional historian and educator in her own right, has shared my life and enthusiasms as well as put up with my many moments of angst. To her I owe more than can be adequately articulated in the last line of these acknowledgments.

—Paul G. Schneider Jr.
Saratoga Springs, New York

Editor's Introduction

Stepping from the Erie Canal packet boat *Albany* to the Schenectady wharf, the young Canadian may have politely nodded his farewell to the two "Yankee girls" he had met and chatted with on the boat and who had struck him as being "rather above the common run of American Belles." Once having landed, his plan was to call on Mr. De Graff, a member of one of Schenectady's prominent political families, but the stagecoach for Albany, his destination, was leaving almost immediately.[1] During the three-hour drive to New York State's capital city, he may have reflected with pleasure and more than a bit of amusement on the incidents of the past two days he had spent on the canal coming east from Utica. The uproar he accidently had caused a few nights earlier, while asleep on board the eastern-bound packet boat *Utica*, had been especially diverting. Reaching Utica early Sunday morning, he had taken passage on the *Albany*, along with a small group of other passengers (including the two young ladies) whose company he had enjoyed.

It was early afternoon that Monday, September 25, 1826, when the stagecoach dropped him off in Albany, where he immediately secured overnight lodging at the Congress Hall hotel. Undoubtedly, he entered his name, Alexander Stewart Scott, and place of residence, Quebec City, in the hotel's guest register. Traveling since early August, the twenty-one-year-old was nearing the end of his trip across the state and heading home.

Popularly regarded as the "chief hotel" in the city, Congress Hall was well situated, providing a commanding view down State Street, the principal thoroughfare of the city. Just across the street was the State Capitol Building, so the hotel also informally functioned as the "headquarters of the legal fraternity, members of the Legislature, and all distinguished travelers."[2] Young Scott was not well known, either in his own country or in the United States, so he wouldn't have been considered "distinguished," but, as a law student soon to become a commissioned lawyer in Quebec, he was part of the legal "fraternity" in Canada. Throughout his trip he had taken every opportunity to observe American legal practices and procedures, comparing them—often unfavorably—with those of British Canada.

Deciding to use the remainder of his afternoon exploring the city, he left the hotel and strolled across the street to the elegantly columned Capitol. He walked through the first-floor Senate and Assembly chambers and then took the stairs to the top floor, where he examined the State Library. An avid reader, he was impressed with what he saw, recording in his journal that the library's book collection, though small, was "very choice."[3] Ascending to the Capitol's roof-top cupola, he marveled at the magnificent view.

When he left the building, he little imagined that 128 years in the future, in 1954, his journal would be purchased by the library he had just visited. He would have been astounded to discover that sixty-five years after its acquisition, it would be published. He had recorded that he undertook the writing of his journal for his own amusement and to share with family and close friends. Had he contemplated its publication, he likely would have polished, revised, cut, and elaborated to create something he felt worthy of a public audience. He was a critical reader and would not have spared himself. Fortunately, none of these things ever happened, so his account remains as lively as when he made the final entry on Sunday, November 19, 1826.

Young Scott

Of the young man who took lodging in the hotel that Monday afternoon in 1826 little is known beyond the barest facts. Alexander Stewart Scott was born on May 18, 1805, in the city of Dundee, located on the River Tay along the east coast of Scotland.[4] His parents, George and Janet Erskine Scott, were both born and raised in Edinburgh, Scotland, and were married there, in the Parish of Saint Cuthbert's, on November 15, 1794.[5] They continued to live in Edinburgh until sometime between 1798, when their daughter, Ann Semple Austin Scott, was born there, and 1801, when their oldest son, Hugh Erskine Scott, was born in Dundee. An entry for a George Scott appears in the 1809 city directory for Dundee, where he apparently was employed as a tailor with a shop located on High Street.[6] Sometime between 1811 (when their youngest son, Robert, was born in Dundee) and 1818, they, along with all their children, immigrated to Canada, apparently first to Halifax, Nova Scotia.[7] In the eight years between 1818 and 1826, the Scott family, through marriage and the pursuit of education and careers, disbursed throughout the Canadian province of Quebec and to the growing community of Palmyra, New York.

When Alexander undertook his journey, his immediate family was comprised of his father, mother, three sisters, and four brothers. It is clear from his journal entries that family was not only important to him, but that they also supported his travels by providing him with welcoming places to stay along the way. To assist readers, the principal members of his family who are mentioned in his journal are briefly identified here. Where others are tangentially referred to by Scott, their identities are provided in the endnotes.

> George and Janet Erskine Scott. Alexander's parents were fifty-two and fifty-five, respectively, in 1826. At the time, George and his wife were living in St. John's, Quebec, where George was employed as a British customs official.
>
> Elizabeth (Betsy) Saunderson Scott. Alexander's youngest sister, seventeen, was living with her parents in St. John's, Quebec.
>
> James Guthrie Scott. Alexander's second-oldest brother, twenty-three, lived in Montreal where he was already practicing law.
>
> Henry (Harry) Stewart Scott. Alexander's younger brother, nineteen, also lived in Montreal. It is unknown whether Henry was in school or working in 1826.
>
> Margaret Jane Scott. Alexander's oldest sister, thirty-one in 1826, was married to William Cunningham Batchelor. Probably sometime after 1821, when the Batchelors' second son, George Scott Batchelor, was born in Quebec City, the family immigrated to the United States and settled in Palmyra, New York, situated on the Erie Canal. William Batchelor was recorded as a merchant on his marriage bond, and it is probable that he continued in that capacity in Palmyra. This supposition is supported by Alexander's journal entries about traveling around the region with him on business.
>
> Ann Semple Austin Scott. Alexander's next-oldest sister, twenty-eight, was living with the Batchelors in Palmyra when Alexander visited them. She married General Walter Grieve of Geneva, New York, on September 17, 1826, while Alexander was still in Palmyra. Grieve, an American veteran of the War of 1812, was himself a Scottish immigrant to the United States.

Even this simple summation of Alexander's family reveals that he came from people striving to firmly establish themselves in the Canadian middle-class of professionals, merchants, and government officials. While far from wealthy, the Scott family was also far from poor. They held responsible positions, and, as Alexander's journal entries make clear, they had contacts within the Canadian medical, legal, merchant, and military communities.

That Alexander himself was adept at meeting influential people and establishing new connections that might prove useful to him in the future is evident throughout his journal. One of its more remarkable aspects is the number of prominent New Yorkers he met and often spoke with at length. Scott struck up conversations with people wherever he went, but they were businessmen, lawyers, judges, doctors, military officers, and public officials whose names and addresses he diligently wrote down because they had shown him courtesies and kindnesses that he hoped to someday repay, or because they might prove to be valuable future contacts for himself or his family. In all his social dealings he was polite and followed the respectful behavior expected of young gentlemen. Being single, he also endeavored to make the acquaintance of the pretty, young ladies he met along the way, but these were clearly eligible women of social standing. He never gives any indication of pursuing or indulging in casual sexual encounters.

Yet, gregarious as he appears, Scott rarely mentions or apparently even "sees," let alone associates with, people who are laborers, poor immigrants, servants, shopkeepers, or anyone who might be below his level of education and middle-class standing. The only exceptions to this are the stagecoach driver on the route to Lewiston, whom he "tips" to enable him to sit on the front seat with the driver and to take the reins for a few miles; the guide taking him below the falls at Niagara; the canal boat captain of the *Utica*; and the owner of the Congress Hall hotel in Albany. These latter two are the only ones he documents by name.

His modes of travel and places of accommodation reflect this unstated, but clearly apparent separation from the common, less-affluent people who are also traveling. This is illustrated by his, what could be construed as callous, observation that on the steamboat he was taking back home to Quebec from Montreal, there were "only two Passengers besides myself on board," when in fact there were forty-five steerage passengers on the same vessel.[8] Scott, of course, was in first class with his own sleeping accommodation. Despite his occasional assertion that he doesn't have much money, virtually every hotel he stays at is advertised as the best in its community. When considering his travel experiences, it is important to remember that in many ways they reflect a different and often separate sphere from those of other less fortunate travelers who are making their way along the same water and land routes at the same time as Scott.

"Passed the best part of the day in reading"

His travel journal also discloses other personal qualities that help define our youthful traveler. For example, his frequent mention of books reveals him to be a keen reader. His journey is barely under way before he confides that he has only a few "not very interesting" books with him to help pass the time. He reads on canal boats, on steamboats, likely in hotels, and when staying with family. His reading ranges from novels to poetry to local newspapers to gazetteers. The fact that while in Albany he visited the State Library and judged its collection as "choice" testifies to his self-defined, critical insights regarding literature and libraries. Reading American author James Fenimore Cooper's most recently published (1826) novel, *The Last of the Mohicans*, he compares Cooper's literary style with that of British author Sir Walter Scott and concludes that Cooper "slavishly" imitated Scott's style of writing.[9] Four years earlier, in its July 1822 issue, *The North American Review*, an American literary magazine, in a lengthy review of Cooper's 1821 novel, *The Spy*, had agreed with Alexander's critical assessment, writing:

> There is no compliment, in that unmeaning adulation, which has styled the author of the Spy the Scott of America; nor do we think public sentiment, in this part of the country [Boston], will bear out a pretension so extravagant. At any rate, for ourselves, we do not hesitate to say, that although uncommon powers are here exhibited, from which we have a right to augur better things, we have discerned nothing in this production which draws the writer a step nearer to the author of the Waverly novels . . .[10]

In the years between 1822 and 1826, better things did come from Cooper's pen, and his novels came to represent an emerging brand of American literary nationalism in a way similar to what Sir Walter Scott's popular historical novels did for Scottish heritage.[11]

Alexander's appetite for books and reading easily was satisfied throughout his journey. Publishers, bookstores, and newspapers flourished in the United States, while in Canada the situation in the opening decades of the nineteenth century was quite different. George L. Parker, in *The Beginnings of the Book Trade in Canada*, convincingly argues that Canada's situation as a British colony created economic and psychological dependence on the mother country that tended to dampen development of its book trade. He further suggests that the long-standing "enmity" between the French- and English-speaking populations of the country, coupled with religious "animosities" among French and English Protestants and Catholics, contributed to the situation. Finally, he asserts that, outside larger urban centers, "pioneer settlements in their isolation tended to be parochial and parsimonious, while the provincial assemblies were reluctant to spend money on schools, libraries and cultural development. To a large extent, reading was an elite preoccupation, and everywhere the wretched state of literacy and education stifled the full benefits of bookselling and printing."[12] Parker also observes that "American books, periodicals, and newspapers always circulated in the provinces . . ."[13] The Canadian printing trade, Parker suggests, owed much of its early existence to American loyalist printers who had fled the United States during and after the Revolution, New England printers, and Scottish printers, who were "the vanguard of an army of Scots and Ulstermen who dominated nineteenth-century printing and bookselling."[14] Alexander's own Scottish heritage, along with his educated middle-class standing, I believe, strongly influenced his obvious love of learning and reading.

During his stay in New York State, Scott discovered that even the Erie Canal packet boats on which he traveled contained, among their furnishings, small libraries with "a pretty good collection of works" available to passengers at a cost of one cent per volume or for nothing at all.[15] His observation suggests that among the population of Canada's neighbor, literacy and reading were not solely confined to the "elite." Indeed, a glance at the front pages of 1826 newspapers of some of the New York communities Scott visited attest to the widespread availability of reading material. If, for example, before he departed the Congress Hall hotel on Tuesday, September 26, he had picked up a copy of the *Albany Argus & Daily Gazette*, he would have seen extensive advertisements for two bookstores, one of which, William Gould & Co., specialized in selling law books. The other, D. Steele & Son's Bookstore, prominently advertised that it had just received "Webster's discourse in commemoration of Adams and Jefferson."[16] This publication was Daniel Webster's *A Discourse in Commemoration of the Lives and Services of John Adams and Thomas Jefferson, Delivered in Faneuil Hall, Boston, August 2nd, 1826*. The deaths of both former presidents, occurring as they did on the fiftieth anniversary of the country's declaring independence from Great

Britain, was a momentous event that provided part of the background against which his trip through New York took place. Alexander had read Webster's speech while in Palmyra and was so impressed with it that he wrote a reminder to himself in his journal "to endeavor to procure a copy to take to Quebec with me."[17] It is just possible that Alexander walked down to Steele's bookstore while still in Albany and purchased a copy to take home. During the time he had spent in Palmyra with his sister and brother-in-law, the local newspaper (the *Wayne Sentinel*) ran an advertisement for Tucker & Gilbert's local bookstore, which boasted that it "intended to keep constantly on hand for sale A CHOICE COLLECTION OF Historical, Theological, Medical, Scientific, & MISCELLANEOUS BOOKS."[18] Its ad also provided an extensive list of titles, among which school books predominated. In nearby Lyons, its newspaper, the *Lyons Advertiser*, for September 20, 1826, printed a listing of books carried by E. J. Whitney's bookstore that took up an entire column.[19]

These examples, selected from locales where Scott stayed and from dates when he was there, hardly provide conclusive evidence of the extent of literacy or reading in the early decades of nineteenth-century New York. They do, however, suggest the availability, at least in communities located on the east-west route of the Erie Canal, of the wide variety of books, periodicals, and newspapers, for which there appears to have been a market sufficiently large and active enough to support the printers, publishers, and bookstore proprietors who offered them for sale. They also give some limited insight into what community booksellers stocked and, therefore, presumably what people in those communities wanted to read. In Palmyra, Tucker & Gilbert's stock included school books ranging from grammars, spellers, atlases, histories, and dictionaries to selections on surveying, astronomy, and philosophy. They also handled an extensive supply of "family medicines," including "Dr. Godbold's Vegetable Balm of Life."[20] E. J. Whitney's bookshop in Lyons tried to draw in customers with titles encompassing both British and American literature (including Sir Walter Scott's popular Waverley Novels), along with histories, biographies, and, of course, Bibles, writing and "cyphering" books, and Webster's spelling books.

In Canada, Alexander, a frequent visitor to his brothers living in Montreal, had access to the flourishing book trade in that city.[21] Also, at home in Quebec City, accessibility to books was provided not only by printer John Neilson, but additionally through an innovative circulating library established by bookseller-journalist Thomas Carey.[22] Whether Alexander took out a subscription to Carey's lending library is not known, but given his enthusiasm for reading, it is entirely possible.

"Went out again to the theatre"

Closely allied with his interest in reading was his love affair with the theater. Over the course of his travels, he details his attendance at six theater performances.[23] At the start of his trip, while in Montreal, he fit in two shows: one on Saturday evening, August 5, and the second on the following Monday, August 7. Montreal's elegant Theatre Royal, which reportedly held approximately a thousand people, had been open less than a year when Scott apparently occupied a seat in its first-tier dress circle (ticket cost: five shillings).[24]

In Palmyra, where he managed to attend three performances and see four plays, the venue was very different. The traveling theater company of "Messrs. Gilbert & Trowbridge" staged its productions in the "assembly room" of Palmyra's St. John's Hotel. The players had announced their performances by placing a prominent advertisement in the *Wayne Sentinel* of Friday, August 18, 1826. In the same issue, the newspaper's publishers commented that the theater company had "lately been playing in Rochester, with good success, and from the reputation of the company, we count upon respectable audiences for them at this place." They went on to note that a production staged the previous evening had attracted a "tolerable house."[25] Alexander, accompanied by his sisters, formed part of the "house" on Monday, August 21, and saw two plays that were, in his opinion, "most cruelly murdered." His critical reaction, however, did not prevent him from accepting gifts of tickets from his brother-in-law, and he attended twice more: on Wednesday, August 23, and Friday, August 25.

Despite his reservations about the quality of acting in the Palmyra productions, Alexander expressed no surprise that theatrical entertainment was available in western New York. As David Grimsted points out in *Melodrama Unveiled: American Theatre and Culture, 1800–1850*, "Drama was a major form of public entertainment available to all classes and the art form most wholly and immediately dependent on popular appeal." It was clearly thriving in 1826, especially in those communities made easily accessible to traveling theater companies by the newly completed Erie Canal. In both Montreal and Palmyra, it was mostly melodrama, penned by British playwrights with "gripping plots leavened by sentimentality and humor," that Alexander saw staged.[26] However, he might have been surprised to discover, as historian Glenn Hughes suggests in his history of American theater, that "the extension of the English-American drama into the wilderness" had its origins in Albany, New York, with the formation of a company of actors specifically recruited to travel and perform in western regions.[27] According to the editors of *The Cambridge History of the American Theater*, "there was little that was fundamentally different between the theatre enjoyed by western spectators and that back east."[28]

Alexander Stewart Scott's passion for the theater evidently lasted throughout his life, as will be seen in the afterword of this book, but in 1826 his travel journal discloses not only his eagerness to go to the theater whenever the opportunity presented itself, but also his fascination with British actor Edmund Kean. Hailed as a brilliant thespian, Kean, especially known for his Shakespearean roles, had risen to stardom on the English stage. During his first tour of North America in 1820, his New York appearance in *Richard III* had garnered popular acclaim, but he "battled with the American press and increasingly was depicted as a problematic, if colorful, figure."[29] Kean launched a return tour to the United States and Canada in 1825, but his erratic behavior, coupled with a widely publicized extramarital affair in England, had damaged his reputation. Scott apparently first witnessed Kean act in Montreal on Saturday, August 5, 1826, and, expecting a performance matching Kean's renown, he was disappointed. Two days later, on Monday, August 7, he again saw the actor and was "much better pleased" with his performance. Just how starstruck Alexander was by Kean is revealed in his journal entry of Monday, October 23, 1826, when, based on a rumor that Kean was traveling by steamboat to New York, he dashed down to the wharf in St. John's, Quebec, to try to see him. The rumor proved false, but however disappointed he may have been, his attachment to the theater remained undiminished.

"Getting on"

Throughout his journal, Scott uses the phrase "getting on" to indicate his progress toward his next destination. That progress was remarkably rapid, perhaps not by twenty-first-century conceptions of speed, but for the second decade of the nineteenth century, it represented a swiftness not previously achievable using earlier forms of overland transport: walking, horseback, heavy wagon, sledge, and sleigh. For example, twenty-one-year-old James D. Bemis, a bookseller employed by an Albany firm, set off for York (now Toronto), Canada, from Albany in late October 1804. In a letter to his sister, Bemis recounted that it took him sixty-two days just to reach Canandaigua, New York, where he decided to settle.[30] He elaborated:

After being detained at Utica, upwards of seven weeks, my patience was so far exhausted, that I determined, notwithstanding the badness of the roads, to make one more attempt to gain the place of my destination; and accordingly hired two wagons to take me to Canandaigua. They had proceeded about fifty rods, when one of them got mired to the hub!—"Good start" you will say. Well! we got out in about an hour, and traveled *eight miles* the first day.[31]

Bemis's experience was extreme, but cross-country travel at any time of year was often challenging and time consuming. Wherever possible, movement by water was preferable. Larger and heavier loads could be carried this way, and under the right circumstances (favorable winds and currents, navigable water depths) water transport was physically easier and faster. While travel in winter was especially difficult, if ice on lakes, rivers, and streams formed to a sufficient depth to support the weight of people, horses, and sledges or sleighs, transport along those routes could continue as conditions allowed.

While the Adirondack and Catskill mountains presented formidable obstacles to easy movement into New York's western regions, the Mohawk River, cutting west from Waterford, where it flows into the Hudson River, provided a narrow opening that proved invaluable to growth and development. Historically, the state's geography has been both an abundant blessing and a bloody curse. Lakes Champlain and George coupled with the Hudson River presented a north-south travel path that had been used for centuries by Native Americans, European explorers, and then the armies of France, Great Britain, Canada, and the United States as they struggled for territorial dominance. What came to be known as the Great Warpath inevitably forced open heretofore largely unexplored (except by Native Americans) lands north and west of the English and American settlements that prior to 1800 were concentrated along the Hudson Valley and not far west of Albany.[32]

It was the needs of armies that resulted in the earliest roads—military roads—being hacked out into those areas of the state still largely a wilderness. Earlier explorers, trappers, traders, woodsmen, missionaries, and daring settlers had moved across the country on trails long used by Native Americans. Moving troops, equipment, supplies, and artillery across the same regions required the construction of something better than paths. While military roads served strategic purposes in wartime, those same roads did not necessarily fulfill civilian needs in peacetime. Archer Butler Hulbert, in his monumental series Historic Highways of America, went so far as to suggest that because of the lack of roads, "the interior of New York was an almost unexplored wilderness at the end of the Revolution in 1783."[33]

Just forty-three years later, when Scott traveled across that same western interior, it was far from an unexplored wilderness. The intervening years had witnessed a series of transforming events that had helped bring about significant changes across the state. One of these events was the 1782 creation by the state legislature of the "New Military Tract," an area of some 1.5 million acres of land in central New York set aside as a land bounty for veterans of the Continental Army. This, along with a growing fever of speculation in western property, fed a pent-up demand for new land to support long-term settlements and regional growth.[34] A second event grew out of the War of 1812, when the federal government learned the hard way that poor roads impede the rapid deployment of troops. With its long border with British Canada, New York was key to America's defense against British invasions from the north. The need to quickly move men and supplies prompted the government to create and fund a military road policy with the aim of improving military mobility and strength.[35]

A greatly improved system of roads was essential to the establishment of successful new communities and corresponding economic expansion. As Secretary of the Treasury Albert Gallatin wrote in his 1808 report to the United States Senate on the importance of roads and canals to the new nation:

> The inconveniences, complaints, and perhaps dangers, which may result from a vast extent of territory, can no otherwise be radically removed, or prevented, than by opening speedy and easy communications through all its parts. Good roads and canals, will shorten distances, facilitate commercial and personal intercourse, and unite by a still more intimate community of interests, the most remote quarters of the United States. No other single operation, within the power of government, can more effectually tend to strengthen and perpetuate that union, which secures external independence, domestic peace, and internal liberty.[36]

Gallatin's words echoed a fundamental concern of earlier federalist supporters of the newly proposed Constitution of the United States, who legitimately worried that without a strong union binding the individual states to each other, those states would ultimately bicker, impose trade barriers against one another, possibly fight one another, and prove easy prey to foreign powers waiting for the entire governmental experiment to collapse. A strong transportation network was seen as, and proved to be, a tangible way to link and bind together the individual states not only with each other, but also with the new territories rapidly being settled to the west.[37] Even some five decades after winning independence from Great Britain, the United States that Scott traveled to was very much a country still struggling to define itself as a nation. Its evolving transportation system was part of that definition.

In New York, some of its earliest roads, like the Great Genesee Road (established by state legislation in 1794 and extended to Lake Erie in 1798), which ran west from Utica through Syracuse, Auburn, and Geneva, and the Ridge Road (1804), linking present-day Rochester with Lewiston, were traversed by stagecoaches similar to those carrying Scott decades later.[38] In the first decades of the nineteenth century, numerous toll roads or turnpikes, which charged their users, were incorporated by the state. By law, these roads were supposed to be constructed to minimal standards aimed at ensuring stable surfaces on which wheeled vehicles could move faster and with less danger of breakdown or delays caused by impassible conditions. D. W. Meinig in his chapter "Geography of Expansion, 1785–1855," writes that by 1821, 278 turnpike companies had been chartered by the state, equaling six thousand miles of roads, "of which two-thirds had actually been built."[39] Writing about the establishment of inns, Katheryne Thomas Whittemore notes that because of the generally slow pace of travel, only limited mileage could be covered in a day, which "resulted in a close spacing of inns. At one time the Ridge Road averaged one inn per mile."[40] All of this, what we today would call infrastructure, facilitated settlers moving west, farmers and merchants shipping their goods and products east to market, and increasingly both foreign and domestic travelers expecting to see the new country and its many scenic wonders.

Concurrently, on the state's lakes and rivers, the invention and practical development of the steamboat revolutionized travel and transport by water. Robert Fulton's steam-powered vessel (originally, simply called by Fulton "the steam-boat") successfully completed its journey between New York City and Albany in August 1807.[41] While this new technology initially suffered from setbacks (mechanical breakdowns and occasional boiler explosions) and from a legal monopoly that limited competition until 1824, steamboats rapidly became more reliable, faster, and safer. Able to navigate against adverse winds and currents, they could maintain dependable departure and arrival schedules—a tremendous advantage to the traveling public. They also became larger, their accommodations for dining and sleeping more comfortable and commodious, and, with increasing competition, their ticket costs more economical.[42]

Less than two years after its introduction on the Hudson River, regular steamboat service began on Lake Champlain between Whitehall, New York, and Saint John's, Quebec, Canada. Interrupted during the War of 1812, that service was quickly reintroduced after peace was declared. In 1817, the Lake George Steamboat Company launched its own regularly scheduled service between Ticonderoga (where passengers from the Lake Champlain vessels could connect to those on Lake George) and Caldwell (today's village of Lake George).[43]

In the summer of 1817 construction of the Erie and Champlain Canals began. For its time, this undertaking by the State of New York was a staggering commitment to radically transforming its transportation infrastructure, and it involved audacious financial and technological risks on a scale never before attempted in the country. When completed in October 1825, the canals provided east-west and north-south seasonal, man-made water passages linking Lake Erie to Albany and Canada to Albany (via Lake Champlain, on which canal boats either sailed or were towed by steam-powered vessels between Whitehall and Canada, and then traveled entirely by canal from Whitehall to Albany).[44] It was a stunning accomplishment and, as intended, it dynamically changed travel across interior New York.

As Carol Sheriff writes in her book *The Artificial River: The Erie Canal and the Paradox of Progress, 1817–1862*, in 1825 alone forty thousand people traveled on the canal's waters.[45] It was an indication of the huge number of passengers who would soon take advantage of the smooth and rapid transit offered by canal boats.

In the late summer and early fall of 1826, as Alexander Stewart Scott made his journey across the state, he benefited from the integration of all the aforementioned transportation changes. Whether by steamboat, stagecoach, ferry, or canal packet boat, his progress was significantly aided by published departure and arrival schedules, along with established points of connection where the traveler could handily change from one form of transport to another better suited to the destination or the traveler's inclination. For example, the Rochester newspaper the *Album*, for Tuesday, August 1, 1826, featured a prominent advertisement in the middle of its front page heralding a "New Line of Stages" that operated from Saratoga Springs to Utica. The line's scheduled route was explicit: "Leaves Wheeler's *Columbian Hotel*, at Saratoga Springs, on Monday, Wednesday and Friday mornings, stopping at [and continuing to list the seven hotels and communities it served] . . . and at the York House in Utica; arriving at the latter place the same evening, where it intersects the Great Western Line of Stages from Albany to Buffalo."[46] Steamboat advertisements providing detailed departure and arrival times between Albany and New York City were spread over the first three pages of the *Albany Argus & Daily City Gazette* for Tuesday morning, September 26, 1826, the same morning that Scott departed the capital city. Page 3 of the same paper carried an extensive advertisement touting the Lake George steamboat *Mountaineer*, the same vessel on which Scott had enjoyed a scenic voyage early in his New York adventure.[47]

In his thought-provoking article " 'Ticketed Through': The Commodification of Travel in the Nineteenth Century," historian Will Mackintosh suggests that "travel was increasingly provided by a capital-intensive service industry that produced a commodity for sale into an expanding market that served a nation that was growing both geographically and demographically." In Scott's travel experiences, I think we can see reflected the beginnings of this trend. Mackintosh believes that travel commodification "happened gradually, partially, and unevenly throughout the nineteenth century . . . ," and he tellingly adds that "individuals' access to commodified travel varied significantly with their race, class, and gender, as well as the varying goals of their travel."[48]

What then was the goal of Scott's travel? Was he heading south into New York as a tourist, joining a growing host of others acting in that role, or did his journey have another purpose? He never clearly articulates why he undertook his trip, although there are hints. His aim was not merely to see the natural beauties of the state, although he was clearly appreciative of them. Fellow passengers aboard the steamboat *Congress* had to convince him to modify his original intention of going straight to Whitehall by detouring slightly to enjoy the scenic splendors offered by an alternate voyage down Lake George. Initially, Scott was worried about the added expense, but he quickly concluded that their advice was well worth it. Having arrived at his sister and brother-in-law's home in Palmyra, he writes that he "began to think of going as far as the Falls of Niagara," but he again has reservations about the cost involved. It seems fair to conclude that as a young student with, in his view, limited finances, he had not embarked on a tour primarily to see the sights.

He obliquely mentions conducting business for his father, and it seems possible that this might have been a purpose for his trip. Since Geneva, New York, and the home of General Grieve was an objective early in his journey, it also is conceivable that—although Scott obviously had never previously met Grieve—some prior business or personal connection had been established by his family with the general. That Grieve already knew Scott's brother-in-law, living just a short distance away from Geneva in Palmyra, is apparent, and since Grieve married Scott's sister Ann just a month later, it seems reasonable to speculate that this impending marriage was another reason for undertaking his trip. It is puzzling, however, that in his journal Scott records very little about this wedding and even seems somewhat surprised by it. With no other family correspondence known to exist from this period, it is impossible to arrive at a definitive conclusion for the reason or reasons for his trip. That he enjoyed his travel, however, is evident. Whatever else, it offered him a welcome break from his law studies and a chance to strike out on his own before settling down to a career. This latter aspect of his trip suggests a faint parallel, of a limited scope and duration, with the established English tradition of young men taking a grand tour of Europe as a culmination of their education before starting their vocations.

The Northern Tour

Probably some of Scott's fellow passengers aboard the steamboat *Mountaineer*—perhaps the very ones who urged him to see Lake George—had embarked on what was popularly called "The Northern Tour." Especially since the signing of the Treaty of Ghent in December of 1814 that had ended the War of 1812 between the United States and Great Britain, traveling for pleasure had become increasingly possible and popular. Richard H. Gassan suggests in *The Birth of American Tourism: New York, the Hudson Valley, and American Culture, 1790–1830* that in addition to its transportation systems, New York's rapidly expanding population, financial wealth, geographic position, and "remarkable scenery," including "some of the country's most sought-after destinations," all contributed to the growth of tourism in the state.[49]

In its September 16, 1826, issue, the *Niles' Weekly Register*, a newspaper reputedly "as well known as the *New York Times* and *Washington Post* are known today," ran an article, titled "Visitors of the North," on that summer's "emigration of the southern citizens to the north" for "health or amusement" and the significant amounts of money spent by those visitors. The anonymous author elaborated on the attractions and popularity of the state of New York:

abounding with the most stupendous and interesting natural and artificial curiosities, and containing the great commercial emporium of the United States, in itself worth a long journey to see; and then her cataracts and falls, mountains and plains, lakes and rivers, mineral and salt springs, canals, roads, bridges, aqueducts, great manufacturing establishments, splendid public institutions, a rich and highly cultivated soil, and a thousand delightful villages, vary the scene and gratify the most wandering fancy.[50]

While Scott did not venture down the Hudson River to visit "the great commercial emporium" of New York City, his travel route adroitly managed to encompass just about every other significant sight listed by the *Register* article. Lakes Champlain and George; Saratoga Springs; the Erie Canal; the fast-growing cities of Syracuse, Rochester, and Buffalo; and Niagara Falls, along with ruins dating from the War of 1812 and the Revolutionary War, all found their way into his travel journal.

Aiding all travelers, but specifically written for tourists, was what Richard Gassan calls a new form of travel literature (other than published, personal travel accounts): the "tourist guidebook." Gassan credits Saratoga Springs, New York, printer Gideon Minor Davidson with publishing America's first tourist guidebook in 1822. Davidson's *The Fashionable Tour: or, A Trip to the Springs, Niagara, Quebeck [sic], and Boston, in the Summer of 1821* "codified and modified a route that had become the accepted path among highly adventuresome travelers prior to the War of 1812."[51] Davidson soon had competitors. Among these was Theodore Dwight, whose guidebook, *The Northern Traveller: Containing the Routes to Niagara, Quebec, and The Springs, with Descriptions of the Principal Scenes, and Useful Hints to Strangers,* was published in 1825. (It is from this publication that the annotated maps used in this book were taken.) Dwight's book promised to provide "all the information of most importance and interest to such as travel for pleasure or health." This included listing the routes and mileage "between all principal places. . . . the best inns. . . . the finest natural scenes . . . and the places which have been rendered memorable by important historical events."[52]

Whether Scott used Dwight's or any of the other similar works available in 1826 is unknown. He might have carried with him any of the following: *A Northern Tour: Being A Guide to Saratoga, Lake George, Niagara, Canada, Boston, &c. &c.,* by Henry Dilworth Gilpin, published in Philadelphia in 1825; *A Pocket Guide, for the Tourist and Traveller, Along the Line of the*

Canals, and the Interior Commerce of the State of New-York, by Horatio Gates Spafford, second edition published in Troy, New York, in 1825; *The Northern Traveller: Containing the Routes to Niagara, Quebec, and The Springs, with the Tour of New-England, and the Route to the Coal Mines of Pennsylvania*, by Theodore Dwight, Jr., published in New York City in 1826; *A Gazetteer of the State of New-York*, by Horatio Gates Spafford, published in Albany, New York, in 1824; or *The Traveller's Pocket Map of New York*, published in Utica, New York, by William Williams in 1826, which also contained a "Canal Guide, for the Tourist and Traveller." What is certain, however, is that he was familiar with or saw a copy of Spafford's 1824 *Gazetteer* because there is a quote almost verbatim from it in his journal.

Guidebook in hand or not, Scott almost certainly benefited from the travel knowledge and advice of his family. As a British customs official stationed at St. John's, Quebec, his father would have been very familiar with the schedules, costs, and details of all the vessels plying Lake Champlain and the Richelieu River. Living and working as a merchant in western New York, his brother-in-law would have been equally familiar with the best travel routes, stagecoach and Erie Canal packet boat lines, and schedules in that region. It is entirely possible that Scott, relying on his family for up-to-date travel information, needed no guidebook with which to direct his way.

Along the main routes of travel—whether on canal, river, lake, or land—accommodations to lodge and feed the increasing numbers of travelers were rapidly established by entrepreneurs who recognized both the growing demand and the profits that could be made meeting that demand. Many of the destinations identified by the travel guides boasted more than a few large inns or hotels. Canal packet boat builders adapted and scaled down the sleeping and eating arrangements of their vessels to provide features that had become synonymous with the much larger steamboats. The confined dimensions of the typical packet boat resulted in clever adaptations, such as the stacked berths that folded up out of the way on both sides of the single central cabin during the day. Many travelers' accounts—including Scott's—comment on these arrangements, sometimes with praise, sometimes with loathing. Whichever the reaction, these floating "hotels" offered by both steamboats and canal packet boats were another innovation that enabled travel by all sorts of people.[53] Indeed, as Colonel William L. Stone of New York City wrote of his own experience on a brand-new Erie Canal packet boat, *The Superior*, not all passengers were "strangers of wealth and taste; . . . ," as Theodore Dwight had assured readers in his 1825 guidebook.[54] Stone recorded in his journal entry for September 21, 1829:

An excellent band of music was on board which had come by invitation from Rochester—it being the first trip of the Superior. The musicians were very respectable young men. But a few of the passengers were so exceedingly vulgar in the eyes of all but themselves, that all on board were rendered uncomfortable. Upstarts, of both sexes, who are innately vulgar, but who have seen just enough of the world to render themselves pert and impudent, who in the consciousness of inferiority are over-anxious to command respect, and who imagine money a substitute for manners, are the most disagreeable travelling companions in existence.[55]

Even the most cursory examination of surviving Erie Canal packet boat passenger lists for 1828–1829 suggests the wide range of people using these vessels. For example, the passenger list for the period from August 11 through September 17, 1828, submitted by packet boat captain Calvin DeGolyer states that among the passengers conveyed on August 13 on his boat were an "Indian & Squaw." He also lists unnamed passengers and the miles he carried them, along with formally named persons such as a Mr. Durling and a Miss Junel.[56] Of course, we have no way of determining the accuracy of this captain's entries (or spelling of names) or those of any of the other surviving passenger lists, but they do suggest two important points. First, the canal packet boats, as with stagecoaches, were egalitarian; anyone with money enough to pay the modest fares could and did ride them. Second, some passengers got on and off the boats after traveling comparatively short distances, indicating that this form of transport was also used simply to get from one place to another within a region. Scott's journal suggests that this is exactly one way his brother-in-law traveled in pursuit of his business interests.

Among the Americans

Just three days after he left Albany, Scott admitted in his journal that he had come "among the Americans a good deal prejudiced against them." Although the War of 1812, between the United States and Great Britain (and, of course, Canada), had been ostensibly over for eleven years, some of the most bitter fighting had taken place in New York and Canada, especially on the Niagara frontier. As historian Alan Taylor observes, "At war's end in Upper Canada, the retreating invaders [Americans] left behind a wasteland of plundered farms and burned mills and villages. . . . The plundering and burning embittered Upper Canadians."[57] The British had returned the favor to the Americans, capturing Fort Niagara in a night bayonet attack and quickly following that up with the destruction of the settlements at Lewiston, Black Rock, and Buffalo.[58] Both sides reaped a bitter harvest of death and destruction, and mutual suspicions continued to linger. The Americans had long entertained the thinly veiled desire to invade, "liberate," and incorporate Canada into the United States. That desire did not end suddenly with peace, and, as Jon Latimer argues, "its repercussions were felt well into the twentieth century."[59]

Still, as soon after the war as June of 1819, there were respectful relations between officers of the previously contending sides. American Captain Roger Jones, accompanying Major General Jacob Brown, commanding officer of the northern division of the army, on an inspection tour, kept a journal of that trip and recorded on June 3 that the Americans visited the British commander of Newark (then called "Niagara"), Upper Canada, which had been "entirely destroyed" by the American army just six years earlier. They were "very politely received" and Jones's wife, Mary Ann, "never having seen British soldiers before, was well pleased with what she saw. The band was ordered to play for our amusement—the music was excellent."[60] Two years later, in her 1821 travel journal, Catharine Maria Sedgwick, touring in the same area of the Niagara region, noted that "the memorials of the War are nearly effaced and all is dressed in smiles of prosperity."[61]

Sedgwick's "smiles of prosperity" in some quarters barely concealed mistrust. The British military forts and garrisons Scott records visiting show the British to be acutely aware of the military threat still posed by the United States facing them across the border in New York State. In April 1825, the British War Department sent a three-person, secret commission composed of Major General Sir James Carmichael Smyth, Lieutenant Colonel Sir George Hoste, and Captain John B. Harris to the United States. Each of these officers had distinguished himself in 1815 at the Battle of Waterloo. They were now entrusted to gather vital intelligence. Back in Great Britain, the officers submitted a written report. Historian James J. Talman, writing in 1933 about this secret military document, concluded that "the most interesting feature of the report is that the possibility of war between the United States and the British American provinces was considered . . . to be very real and that they thought a plan of attack on the United States might well be drawn up."[62] That plan of attack, suppressed in their published report, included targeting key structures of the Erie Canal, such as the aqueduct at Rochester, with the strategic purpose of impeding movement of American military supplies to Lakes Erie and Ontario. Obviously, these secret invasion plans were never implemented, but the spying mission into New York State resulting in their formulation provides some indication of the extent of military tensions between the two nations.

However much or little those tensions were evident to the common citizen of either country, the relics, crumbling fortifications, battlegrounds, burial sites, and memorials dating from past conflicts abounded. As Thomas A. Chambers observes in *Memories of War: Visiting Battlefields and Bonefields in the Early American Republic*, "Battlefields where Americans had fought to win and maintain their independence, whether in 1776 or 1812, provided an ideal venue for reflecting on not just valiant struggle and martial glory, but also emotional responses to landscape and memory."[63] Nor was it just Americans who experienced such responses, as Scott testifies by his own account of wanting to visit the Canadian memorial to the British hero of the Battle of Queenston Heights, Major General Sir Isaac Brock.

While Scott and his family had not immigrated to Canada until after the end of the war and, so far as is known, were not directly affected by the North American conflict, as British citizens they very likely experienced the wider implications of Britain's simultaneous war with France. They also must have been exposed to anti-American propaganda. As his journal makes clear, Scott was proud of his Scottish heritage and was certainly pro-British.

The United States he traveled to was not simply a foreign, recently antagonistic adversary, it was also a country of thriving business, expansion, and opportunity to which two of his sisters and their families had themselves immigrated. On some personal level he must have felt his allegiances torn. Americans, and especially New Yorkers, in 1826 were in a celebratory mood. The Erie Canal was in its first year of full operation from Buffalo to Albany and was proving to be a tremendous commercial and financial success. New settlers, merchants, entrepreneurs, and businessmen were flowing into the state along its path. The country was celebrating its fiftieth anniversary of independence and was feeling more assured of its ability to hold its own against any foreign power wishing to interfere with its future. Just the year before, in 1825, the Marquis de Lafayette, French hero of the American Revolution, had returned to make a grand tour of the rapidly expanding country. As Laura Auricchio points out in *The Marquis: Lafayette Reconsidered*, his reception proved to be "the grandest celebration the young nation had ever seen." In every community he visited, people turned out to see and honor him. "He was a living embodiment of the nation's founding principles, and his enduring vitality augured well for the future of his adopted land."[64] This vitality was especially welcome given the deaths of former presidents and founding fathers Thomas Jefferson and John Adams on Independence Day in 1826. America was maturing and feeling its strength and New York State was helping lead the way forward.

Scott's self-admitted prejudices against Americans are largely absent from his journal entries. Certainly, he mocks what he perceives as the ignorance of law students being examined in Utica, the clothes and tobacco-chewing habit of a presiding judge in Troy, and the slapdash militia units he watches drilling, but rarely are his comments cruel or written in anger. It is only the preaching of hellfire Presbyterian ministers he encounters that moves him closest to outright anger.

However, he exhibits other prejudicial stereotypes typical of the period. For example, he gleefully repeats an Irish joke emphasizing the commonly held gullibility of that nationality. He also accepts without comment or question the characterization of the founder of a proposed Jewish settlement on Grand Island as "cracked in the upper story."[65]

In general, however, he remains open to seeing America on its own terms, a characteristic, I believe, that enabled him to arrive at the conclusion toward the end of his journey that most of his bad feelings about Americans had been "done away with," and to add that he had allowed his prior views to be shaped by other Canadians, a mistake he would not make again.[66] This is a remarkable admission and suggests a strong sense of self-awareness, a willingness to admit when he is proven wrong, and an openness of opinion and judgment, all characteristics that make Scott's travel entries engaging and historically valuable.

Everything Worthy of Observation

Scott uses the phrase, "everything worthy of observation," or a variation of that wording, throughout his journal to emphasize the noteworthiness of a scene or phenomenon that he found especially intriguing. It is a defining characteristic of his travel account. Naturally, those things Scott finds of interest, while differing from other individuals' travel accounts according to personal tastes, perspectives, backgrounds, class, gender, and nationality, are also influenced by widely shared, early nineteenth-century cultural ways of seeing the world. For example, Scott used the term "picturesque" when he recorded his reaction to the scenery on the Erie Canal at Little Falls. At

Niagara Falls he wrote that "the sublimity of the scene baffles all description," and he quoted from the poetry of Lord Byron, the great Scottish-born poet of his era, to help express his own impressions of what he sees there. As Raymond J. O'Brien explains in *American Sublime: Landscape and Scenery of the Lower Hudson Valley*, no descriptive terms were repeated so often and with such significance by nineteenth-century writers and travelers than "sublime" and "picturesque."[67] He elaborates: "Sublimity was said to be present when a landscape reflected the more vehement or violent aspects of nature."[68] O'Brien continues, "The picturesque required that a landscape be irregular in detail, rough, coarse in surface texture, variegated in color shading, or perhaps complex and intricate in pattern."[69] Originating in Europe and applied by travelers to the landscape there, these descriptive concepts were soon adopted to depict the American landscape as well.[70] Their influence is clear in Scott's evocative writing.

It is also worth keeping in mind that what Scott elects to write in his travel journal is influenced by his interests, youth, curiosity, social and cultural background, education, and other, less-obvious factors, like his day-to-day health and mental state. Things that affect each of us every single day, whether we are aware of them or not, and have great influence over what we see, what we perceive as important and worth recalling, and our emotional responses to the places, events, situations, and people we encounter. These are the very elements that make travel accounts, whether over 190 years old like Scott's, or just recently published, a source of never-ending fascination and interest.

With his decision to keep a journal of his travels, Scott was hardly unique among his Canadian and American contemporaries. In his survey of diary literature, Steven E. Kagle states, "The diary is one of the oldest literary forms written in America. The large numbers of surviving diaries kept by the early settlers is just one indication of how highly they and their descendants valued the practice."[71] Of course, it also exemplifies a high rate of literacy. Kagle enumerates the types of colonial diaries typically kept, breaking them down into spiritual, travel, romance and courtship, war, and situational diaries (that is, those that were undertaken to record a particular situation in which the diarist found her- or himself).[72] Of colonial travel diaries he observes: "Whether journeying for pleasure, health, or business, these travel diarists tried to record experiences that, when compared to those they had had at home, might confirm or redirect but rarely repudiate the values of their societies."[73] In characterizing the differences between eighteenth- and nineteenth-century diaries, Kagle asserts that the latter reveal a greater sophistication of language and "were more likely to mix elements of the diary of external incident with those of the introspective journal."[74] He also offers the fascinating conclusion, based on his reading of "thousands" of diaries, "that there is no such thing as a private diary. I am inclined to believe that almost all, if not all, diarists envision an audience for their entries."[75] In "Books, Reading, and the World of Goods in Antebellum New England," Ronald Zboray and Mary Zboray add the compelling observation that as "well-educated middle class families . . . contended with the often dolorous by-products of abundance and capital accumulation—upheaval, mobility, and estrangement from friends and family—they turned to letter writing and diary keeping. Such literary efforts helped them maintain their past connections and to preserve memories of their unfolding lives."[76]

Within Alexander Stewart Scott's travel journal can be found specific reflections of the more generalized characteristics of journals and diaries sketched in the preceding paragraph. In his case, he was clear about his intended audience: it was his family and a few friends. As Kagle suggests, however, Scott also wrote for himself, not merely for his own amusement, as he somewhat dismissively quips, but I believe as a personal record of his memories and reflections on his journey and the significant role it played in his young life in late 1826.

There is one other consideration when endeavoring to place Scott's journal into sharper perspective. Author Tony Horwitz, when comparing the journals kept by Captain James Cook and botanist Joseph Banks on the same eighteenth-century voyage, observes that Captain Cook left out "many details of ship life that to him seemed routine," while Banks's entries were more personal and elaborative.[77] Part of this difference of approach can be attributed to the differences in the writers' respective positions of responsibility and, of course, to their individual personalities. However, what is important to note in relation to the contents of Scott's journal— or that of any other travel journal—is that those things that are typically commonplace to the writer are often viewed as unremarkable. Being taken for granted, they simply are not recorded. In Horwitz's example, Cook's and Banks's journals complement each other, filling in what the other may have left out, offering differing perspectives, because what is unimportant to one, is very important to the other. Scott's travel journal adds yet another valuable perspective to our cumulative understanding of early nineteenth-century New York and Lower Canada, a perspective that is rich in those details that caught his attention and a perspective that adds fresh information complementing previously published travel accounts.

Provenance and Authenticity

Every diary depends for its survival on the goodwill of family, friends or executors, together with the whims of chance.

—Mark Bostridge, "Life on the Wing"

The survival of Alexander Stewart Scott's remarkable travel journal tenuously depended on each of the elements of chance so well stated in the preceding epigraph. The story of that survival is an integral part of its history and authenticity. The chain of ownership of any historic object, be it a work of art, a vintage automobile, or an 1826 manuscript, is known as provenance.

Presently, the complete provenance of Scott's journal can only be partially reconstructed. Upon his death, we might speculate that it, along with his other possessions, passed to his lawful heirs. However, unless a last will and testament is found that specifically mentions the journal, or a probate inventory of his estate is located, in which the journal was enumerated, that assumption cannot be validated. Instead, we must turn to the physical evidence, scant though it is, that the journal itself offers as clues of its subsequent ownership. There are two handwritten inscriptions on the inside of its front cover. In pencil at the top appears: "Journal of a tour in the Eastern states by Stewart Scott of Quebec." Comparing the handwriting with that of the journal proper, it seems likely that Scott wrote this himself; he often used his second name, Stewart, instead of his first name. Below this, written in ink toward the center of the page, appears: "H. C. Scott, Montreal." These initials probably are those of Henry Castle Scott (1843–1912), a nephew. Following several blank pages at the front of the bound volume, on the top of the seventh page, appears the signature of Henry S. Scott, also written in ink. This is most likely Henry Stewart Scott (1807–1883), one of Alexander Stewart Scott's younger brothers (referred to as "Harry" in the journal), who also lived and died in Quebec City, Quebec, Canada. One further bit of evidence is presented by the journal. At the top of the third blank page from the front, written in pencil, are the words: "55 years ago Stewart then 21." Since the journal was penned in 1826, the year Scott was twenty-one years old, this inscription would have been jotted down in 1881. Based on these admittedly unsubstantiated bits of evidence, I believe it probable that, after Alexander Stewart Scott's death, the ownership of the journal remained in the immediate family and, at some point, was in the possession of Henry Stewart Scott, who either gave it or willed it to *his* son (and Scott's nephew), Henry Castle Scott. While Henry Castle Scott and his wife, Jessie Cassels Scott (née Wyld), had four children of their own who conceivably might have inherited the journal, any record of actual ownership goes cold between Henry Castle Scott's death in 1912 and 1954, when the New York State Library purchased the 8¼ x 5 1/8 inch, 136-page journal from a local book dealer and added it to its manuscripts and special collections holdings.[78]

This provenance, speculative though it is until 1954, strongly suggests that the journal remained in Scott family hands for at least eighty-six years and possibly longer. Provenance helps support authenticity, and the evidence presented by examination of the journal itself and cited in the preceding paragraph tends to support the conclusion that it is authentic to its period and attributed author. There are no known surviving specimens of Scott's handwriting with which to compare the handwriting of the journal. However, the fact that Scott's name appears in contemporary Canadian steamboat passenger records on the precise dates he records in his journal offers strong corroborative evidence that he was indeed its author.

Looking at the handwriting, which is strong, legible, and surprisingly free from the sort of variations one might expect to find in travel notes jotted down while in motion, suggests two possibilities. The first is that he wrote up each entry after he had stopped for the day or was in a place free from movement or distractions. The second is that the present journal is not the one he actually kept while on the road, but a fair copy made once he had returned home to Quebec City. The truth about which of these possibilities is accurate may never be known, but regardless, its originality, I believe, remains unchallenged.

Once the journal was acquired by the State Library, it rested there safely, but little known, until 2015, when a University at Albany doctoral student in history, Matthew DeLaMater, rediscovered it while conducting his own research and recognized its unique importance.[79] Soon thereafter, I undertook an initial transcription of the journal to which I added explanatory notes. For this publication, those notes have been significantly revised; additionally, an introduction and afterword have been written to provide some basic historical context for the journal.

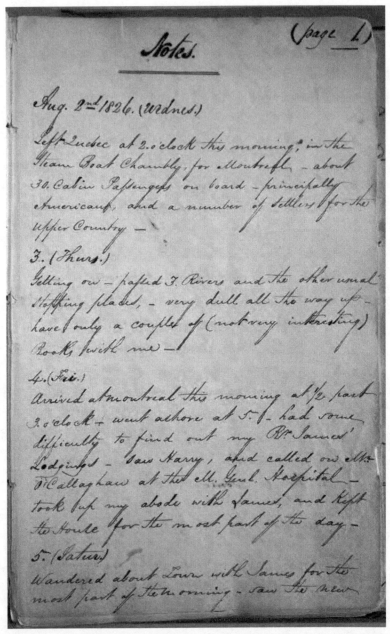

Figure I.1. Original first page of Alexander Stewart Scott's 1826 travel journal. New York State Library call number BD13145. Courtesy of the New York State Library, Manuscripts and Special Collections.

Transcribing the Original Journal

While Scott's dated entries run consecutively with no breaks, the decision was made early in the publication process to divide the journal into nine chapters. Each chapter covers a portion of his trip and is introduced with a short paragraph placing it in geographic context. Following the nine chapters and afterword are two appendices. The first of these is a list of the names and addresses of people he met during his journey whom he wished to remember. The second is a meticulous record of his expenses, the types of transportation he used, and the miles he traveled, all neatly recorded in column format at the back of his journal.

Naturally, the original travel journal was handwritten. While remarkably legible, there are instances where words, abbreviations, and other writing practices, common to the early nineteenth century, present barriers to easy, modern comprehension. To explain exactly how each of these has been addressed, the transcription guidelines outlined here were followed throughout the process of preparing the printed text from the original.

The guiding principle of this transcription has been to intervene with the original manuscript as little as possible. Where interventions were necessary, they have been made in the interests of clarity and understanding.

Punctuation. Scott's original punctuation is retained, including the frequent use of dashes to separate seemingly complete sentences or to indicate breaks in the flow of his recorded thoughts and impressions. Exceptions to this rule include: (a) a period silently replaces a dash where Scott clearly intended a new sentence or paragraph; (b) where clarity of meaning is improved by proper punctuation rather than the original dash, that punctuation is silently inserted. The reader should bear in mind that Scott very probably penned his journal entries spontaneously with little thought or regard to proper punctuation. Further, rules governing punctuation have changed dramatically in the intervening years; allowance must be made for Scott's seemingly lackadaisical and often inconsistent punctuation.

Spelling. Scott's original spelling is retained. Occasionally, words seem misspelled because of (a) differences in British and American spelling (e.g., theatre for theater) and (b) differences between nineteenth- and twenty-first-century spelling (e.g., waggon for wagon). In such instances, Scott's original spelling is retained. There are other cases in which he spells a word as it sounds such as "birth" for "berth," meaning a place on which to sit or sleep. In these occurrences, the modern spelling follows the original in brackets the first time it appears in the text (e.g., birth [berth]).

Capitalization. A common practice of early nineteenth-century writers, including Scott, was to capitalize words seemingly indiscriminately within sentences. This practice, long out of use today, had its origins as far back as the sixteenth century and, over the intervening centuries, evolved into using capital letters "at the beginning of every sentence, proper name, and important noun." Still later, "some writers began using a capital for any noun they felt to be important." Scott's use of capitals probably falls into this latter category. In any case, his practice is retained wherever such capitalization does not obstruct the reader's understanding. In those instances where the capitalization of a word could cause confusion, it is silently corrected.[80]

Underlined words. Scott often uses single or double underlining of words to indicate special emphasis. In all cases these are retained and duplicated in the printed text.

Placement of periods after numerals. For some yet-undetermined reason, Scott very often (but not always) placed a period after any numeral (e.g., 4. PM and 25. miles). These can be confused with modern punctuation, so in all cases these extraneous periods have been silently removed. It should also be noted that Scott is inconsistent in his method of recording numbers and fractions, sometimes writing them out and sometimes expressing them as numerals. Instead of changing the format of his numbers to one or the other form, both are retained in this transcription.

Abbreviations. Scott uses many abbreviations, which, while commonly understood in the early nineteenth century, can create stumbling blocks for modern readers. Therefore, the equivalent modern meaning or definition of an abbreviation is provided in brackets the first time that abbreviation appears in the text. (e.g., Cap$^{tn.}$ [captain]). Where an abbreviation remains the same in modern usage, no explanation is offered (e.g., M^r is clearly understandable as Mr.).

Indecipherability of one or more words. In those few instances where one or more words are indecipherable in Scott's handwriting, that is indicated in brackets following the word or words (e.g., [one word indecipherable] and [two words indecipherable]).

Deleted word or words. Occasionally, Scott crosses out one or more words where he has made a correction, revision, or deletion. These have been retained in the printed text. Where the original text he crossed out can be deciphered, it is inserted in brackets after the deleted word.

Redundant words. Occasionally, when his entry extended from the bottom of one page to the top of the next, Scott repeated the same word twice. Very rarely, he has done the same thing within a sentence. In either case, the redundant word has been silently eliminated.

Date and day of journal entries. Throughout, Scott included the day and date on which he wrote each entry. A typical instance would be: 18 (Fri.). To make the date of each entry clearer, the day, month, and date have been inserted in italics above the entry, replacing Scott's abbreviated dating scheme (e.g., *Friday, September 22nd*).

Archaic words. Predictably, with the passage of almost two centuries since Scott composed his journal entries, the meaning of some English words and terms have changed or entirely dropped out of common usage. Unsurprisingly, he occasionally uses a French phrase or a Scottish term. Throughout this transcription, notes have been added to assist the reader by offering definitions for archaic words, Scottish terms, and French phrases. Unless otherwise noted, these definitions are taken from the *OED Online* (*Oxford English Dictionary*), Oxford University Press. The abbreviations s.v. and s.vv., which stand for sub verbo and sub verbis (plural), are used in definition entries to denote the word or words under which the definition given is located. It is also used in encyclopedia entries to identify the name or phrase under which the entry may be found.

Illustrations

Scott's original journal contains no sketches or drawings. His written entries were sufficient to conjure the mental images of what he had personally seen. Modern readers have no such advantage. Even if one or more locations or landmarks mentioned by Scott remain familiar today, like Niagara Falls for instance, much has changed since 1826. Therefore, many illustrations, contemporary to the early nineteenth century, have been added to this published version of his journal. These broadly fall into two categories. In the first, maps from Theodore Dwight's 1825 travel guide, *The Northern Traveller*, have been included and annotated to graphically suggest the travel routes he followed in the different stages of his trip. In the second, carefully selected engravings, watercolors, sketches, and early photographs have been added with the intent of helping readers visualize some of the specific places Scott mentions. Whenever possible, images dating from the 1820s or 1830s were chosen. Certainly, an artist's selection and representation of a particular scene is no less subjective than what Scott, or any other diarist, decided to write about, but nonetheless these illustrations provide us with strong visual clues of early nineteenth-century New York and Lower Canada. It is also worth noting that the subjects artists chose to depict both contributed to and reflected the rapidly growing popularity of the natural, man-made, and historical sights of New York State.

Notes

> . . . the footnote has been for centuries an indispensable tool of the scholar and a source of endlessly varied delight for the layperson.
>
> —Chuck Zerby, *The Devil's Details: A History of Footnotes*

My hope is that my notes, found just before the index at the back of this publication, provide both supplemental explanatory information along with occasional delight and surprise that will enhance the reading experience of Scott's journal for all readers. Simply stated, these notes serve three functions. First, as explained in the transcription guidelines, many provide definitions of archaic words or terms used by Scott. Second, whenever possible they identify people or places that Scott mentions. Third, while his travel account can be enjoyed without reference to any of the explanatory notes, they frequently elaborate on a topic or an event to which Scott refers.

The 1826 New York State Travel Journal of Alexander Stewart Scott

Preface

In November 1826, after returning to Canada from his lengthy journey through New York State, Scott jotted down a preface to his written account of the trip. It is only appropriate that he introduce his journal in his own words.

Preface!
Gentle, or <u>Courteous</u> Reader! (which ever of these Titles may please thee most).

As this journal or Diary, (by seafaring Men yclept[1] a "Log Book"), was never intended for more than the perusal of two or three Friends and Relations, and by no means expected to meet the eye of a <u>Critic</u>, or of a <u>would</u> <u>be Critic</u>, the <u>Author</u> (!) hopes that it will be perused with all due indulgence to the many faults which it no doubt contains.

> For the great unknown
> (signed) Jean Bte Malars habal-baz[2]
> Editor &c.

<u>November</u> <u>1826</u>

Chapter One

"Left Quebec at 2 o'clock this morning . . ."

With the new day of August 2, 1826, only two hours old, Alexander Stewart Scott leaves his home in the city of Quebec, Canada, for a trip that will last over three months and take him through the heart of New York State. As he makes his way, first west to Montreal, then south to St. John's (now called Saint-Jean-sur-Richelieu), Quebec, Canada, he stays with family members before beginning his journey by steamboat down Lakes Champlain and George and by coach from Caldwell Village (now called Lake George Village) to Schenectady.

Wednesday, August 2nd
    Left Quebec at 2 o'clock this morning, in the Steam Boat Chambly, for Montreal — about 30 Cabin Passengers on board — principally Americans, and a number of settlers for the upper Country.[1]

Thursday, August 3rd
    Getting on — passed 3 Rivers and the other usual stopping places, — very dull all the way up — have only a couple of (not very interesting) Books with me.[2]

Friday, August 4th
    Arrived at Montreal this morning at ½ past 3 o'clock — went ashore at 5 — had some difficulty to find out my Br. [Brother] James' Lodgings — saw Harry, and called on M^r. O'Callaghan at the M. [Montreal] Genl. Hospital — took up my abode with James, and Kept the House for the most part of the day.[3]

Saturday, August 5th

Wandered about Town with James for the most part of the morning — saw the new French Catholic Church[4] — and left a card & a Letter of Introduction to a Mr. Fremont (from Mr. Burroughs).[5] Went to the Theatre in the evening with O'Callaghan, and saw the far favored Kean, as Sir Edward Mortimer in the play of "The Iron Chest."[6] Certainly as far as I am able to judge, a most able Performer — but must confess that (at least in this character) he fell much short of the high flown expectations I had formed of him, from the almost unqualified praise lavished on him by every person of my acquaintance in Montreal (not a few) who had seen him — am sorry did not arrive in time to see him in Othello, which I would conceive to be a piece infinitely more calculated for a proper display of his talent. A good number of Ladies & Gent^m. [Gentlemen] from Quebec in the House — some of whom I knew.

Sunday, August 6th

Passed the whole of to-day at home, my Br. Harry called and kept me company — rather lonely towards the evening — dressed, — but prevented from going out by Rain, which for about an hour fell in torrents — James went to spend the Evening at <u>McCords</u> — did not go myself although invited — went to Bed early, after drinking a glass of good Punch.[7]

Monday, August 7th

Rose late — called on O'Callaghan, and about 11 AM went with James to Court (K.B.)[8] to observe the proceedings at the <u>Enquête</u> sittings[9] — with a very few exceptions, I think the system of doing law business generally far superior in Quebec — a great deal of noise and confusion in the Court Hall — where <u>all</u> the Enq. [Enquêtes] are taken — went again to the Theatre this evening where Kean appeared as Sir Giles Overreach in "a New Way to pay old Debts"[10] — much better pleased with him in that character — good scenery — a great number of Ladies in the dress Circle (where I was) can't say the L. [ladies] of Montreal are much to my taste, either as it regards personal attractions, or manners — but have not the pleasure of knowing many of them — the young Men, generally speaking, either <u>real</u> or imitation Bucks[11] — far however from being of the <u>first water</u>[12] — what I have heard said of the Inhabitants of M. is I think (at least partly) true, i.e. that they are stiff, unsocial, and much given to useless Ceremony, even in their intercourse with one another.

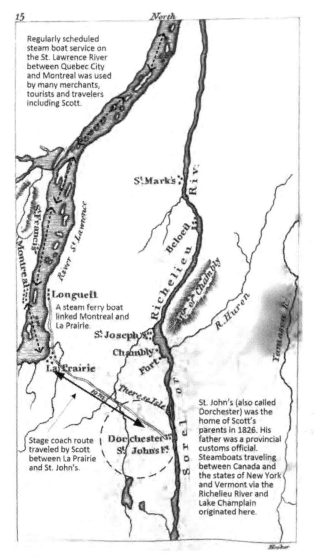

15 North

Regularly scheduled steam boat service on the St. Lawrence River between Quebec City and Montreal was used by many merchants, tourists and travelers including Scott.

St. Mark's

Richelieu Riv.

S. Francis

Montreal

River St Lawrence

Beloeil R.

Longueil

A steam ferry boat linked Montreal and La Prairie.

Mt. of Chambly

R. Huren

S. Joseph

Chambly

Fort

La Prairie

Therese Isle

Stage coach route traveled by Scott between La Prairie and St. John's.

Dorchester

St. John's Ft.

Sorel or

St. John's (also called Dorchester) was the home of Scott's parents in 1826. His father was a provincial customs official. Steamboats traveling between Canada and the states of New York and Vermont via the Richelieu River and Lake Champlain originated here.

Map 1.1. Detail of the region around St. John's and Montreal, Quebec, Canada, annotated to show the variety of transport and the route Scott took at the start and the end of his journey to New York State. The original is "Map 15, St. John's / Montreal, Canada," from [Theodore Dwight], *The Northern Traveller: Containing the Routes to Niagara, Quebec, and The Springs, with Descriptions of the Principal Scenes, and Useful Hints to Strangers* (New York: Wilder & Campbell, 1825). Courtesy of the New York State Library, Manuscripts and Special Collections.

Tuesday, August 8th

Rose early, and called on several persons on business — saw my Br. Harry and at 10 AM set off for Laprairie in the Steam Ferry Boat — a very strong current in this part of the ~~Course~~ River[13] — arrived at L. [La Prairie] about mid-day where I saw the Rev^d. [Reverend] Mr. Baldwyn, Pastor of St. Johns,[14] and a Mrs. McCallum, on their way to Montreal — had a long talk with the Rev^d. — started with the Stage for St. J. [Saint John's[15]] which we reached at 4 PM — a good carriage — but rather rough Roads — found my Family all well, and intend staying with them for a few days previous to my departure for the States, where I will probably remain for 3 or 4 weeks.

Wednesday, August 9th

Very warm, and but few inducements to stir out — passed the best part of the day in reading — and the pleasant company of my Mother & Sister[16] — introduced by the latter to her Friend Miss Baldwyn (Daughter of the Gentleman I met at Laprairie) a young Lady of pleasant, but rather reserved manners.[17]

Thursday, August 10th

Walked out with my Father[18] towards the Garrison,[19] and spent an hour with great pleasure with him — towards the afternoon my Br. Harry arrived to spend his Birth Day with us — passed a delightful evening at home — sweet to recall old scenes to recollection — felt completely happy.

Friday, August 11th

After Breakfast Harry and I went a canoeing — with some trouble got a small mast & Sail fixed up, and in cruizing [cruising] about got through the Forenoon very happily — read the most part of the afternoon, and in the evening after Tea we all went out together for a walk — early to Bed.

Saturday, August 12th

Nothing particular to observe — spent my time much the same as yesterday — purpose [propose] to start by the St. Bt. [steamboat] Congress on Monday Morning for Whitehall on my way to the Upper Country.[20]

Sunday, August 13th

Excessively warm, went to Church in the morning with all the Family, to hear the Rev^d. Mr. Baldwin[21] — a very neat, well finished off [illegible word crossed out] Building, but by no means crowded to excess — my

Mother taken with a sudden fit of sickness — (no service in the afternoon) — Miss Baldwyn called in the evening and took Tea with us en famille[22] — and afterwards joined us all in a walk — really a very pleasant, sensible Girl, & improves wonderfully upon acquaintance — took a Berth on board of the Congress, & saw Miss B. home.

Monday, August 14th
Rose this morning at ½ past 4 — packed up my things — went out to bathe, accompanied by Harry — and about 8 AM (after having breakfasted,) left St. Johns in the St. Bt.[23] — every appearance of favorable Weather — passed the Isle aux Noix[24] about 11 o'clock — about 1 PM opposite Rouse's Point, a piece of land stretching out a good way in the Lake — the Americans had built a very fine large stone Fort upon this Point, but by the last settlement of the Boundary Line, it was found out to have been erected on British Property[25] — the village of Champlain lies close by — stopt at Plattsburgh and Port Kent in passing — the places in themselves poor enough in appearance, but the Country round about delightful — a small storm, the Boat rolled about just like a ship at sea — a few of the Passengers sick — arrived at Burlington about 7 PM where we stopt for about half an hour — went ashore and walked up the Village & purchased some very fine Pears — much pleased with the general fine appearances of the Country at this place — a short distance beyond B. [Burlington] a large bare Rock[26] appears in the Lake, perhaps 30 feet above the surface of the Water — a singular sight. Begin to be quite undetermined whether I shall go on to Whitehall &c, or take the Rout [route] of Lake George — much tempted by the report of several of my Fellow Passengers of the fine scenery, to choose the latter — but which will detain me one day longer on my Journey, and I believe cost more money, (of which, alas! my stock is not too great) — Passed Essex and Chimney Point in the course of the evening, both villages sit.[d] [situated] on the Banks of the Lake — arrived at a place called Shoreham about 3 in the morning of the 15 [fifteenth] where I went on shore with several others, having determined to go on by Lake George — and got a Bed at the only Tavern in the Village.

Tuesday, August 15th
Crossed the River about 8 AM to Ticonderoga, and proceeded (10 of us!) in a stage to the place of embarkation at ~~Lake George~~ the Lake.[27] Shoreham is in the state of Vermont & Ticonderoga in that of New York — the Dollar in the first has 6, and in the latter, 8 shillings of the American

Map 1.2. Annotated map detail of Lake Champlain showing the approximate route of the steamboat *Congress*, on which Scott booked passage during both his trip into New York State and his return home to Quebec. The original is "Map 14, Lake Champlain," from [Theodore Dwight], *The Northern Traveller: Containing the Routes to Niagara, Quebec, and The Springs, with Descriptions of the Principal Scenes, and Useful Hints to Strangers* (New York: Wilder & Campbell, 1825). Courtesy of the New York State Library, Manuscripts and Special Collections.

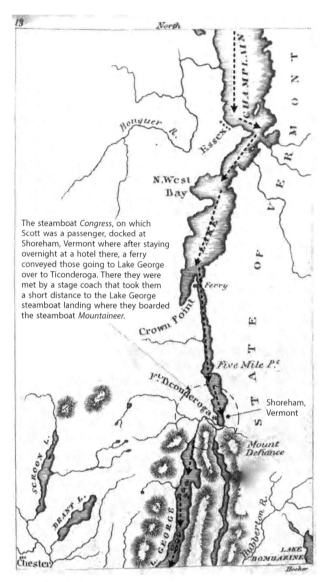

The steamboat *Congress*, on which Scott was a passenger, docked at Shoreham, Vermont where after staying overnight at a hotel there, a ferry conveyed those going to Lake George over to Ticonderoga. There they were met by a stage coach that took them a short distance to the Lake George steamboat landing where they boarded the steamboat *Mountaineer*.

Shoreham, Vermont

Map 1.3. Map detail of Lakes Champlain and George annotated to suggest the approximate route of Scott's travel down both lakes by steam-powered boats. The original is "Map 13, lakes Champlain and George," from [Theodore Dwight], *The Northern Traveller: Containing the Routes to Niagara, Quebec, and The Springs, with Descriptions of the Principal Scenes, and Useful Hints to Strangers* (New York: Wilder & Campbell, 1825). Courtesy of the New York State Library, Manuscripts and Special Collections.

money — when informed I had to pay 6/ [/ is the symbol for shillings] at S. [Shoreham] I told the <u>Host</u> I would settle with him when I got over the Ferry, and he, not suspecting any thing agreed to it — accordingly when we had crossed I offered him a Dollar & demanded 2/ change — the Fellow's look of surprise, and exclamation at the trick were really laughable, I of course did not insist on the difference, but, it occasioned a laugh to myself & Fellow Passengers, to several of whom I had previously communicated my design — got on board of a small Steam Boat called the "Mountaineer,"[28] and started about 10 AM — went below, where I shaved and dressed — getting on — the most romantic & beautiful scenery I ever beheld in my life — had heard much of the beauties of the place, but the reality exceeds my most sanguine expectations — worth while for any person to travel 500 miles just to have the pleasure of passing through this Lake — all the Passengers on board who have not already been here, quite in raptures about it. Immense mountains piled on one another rising from the waters edge, some 1000, 1200, and even 1500 feet high above the surface of the Lake — here and there is one quite perpendicular — the smallest fogs hide the heads of the more distant ones, and light clouds are generally seen sailing along the whole range — the Lake is very serpentine, and the different <u>perspectives</u>, as viewed from the various and many turnings, almost (at least with me) baffle all description — 12 o'clock — opposite "Sabbath day Point," a small piece or tongue of flat Land shelving out into the water — the only <u>low</u> piece of ground to be seen at this place, during the Revolutionary War, Lord Amherst and his army, landed upon a Sunday morning, while upon their way to Fort Wm Henry, and breakfasted — from which circumstance it got its name[29] — about ¾ of a mile further on is "Black Mountain" — the summit of which is <u>2200</u> feet above the level of the water, which is close at its foot — 1 PM — half way through the Lake — at a place called the "Narrows" where a large cluster of small romantic Islands lie right in the <u>middle</u> of the Lake — the channel taken by the <u>Steamer</u> is not perhaps more than 25 yards in width — there are two islands hereabouts called the "Twins," both of the same shape and size, and so close to one another that a man of moderate activity might leap across — a canoe, (with a man on board engaged in fishing) lying between them, <u>stern</u> or <u>stem</u> — mountain just opposite, of a very dark, dismal appearance, almost black — 1700 or 1800 feet high — the most part of the mountains, more particularly on the left hand side (going up) quite bare in some places, or only partially covered with a few wretched stumps of pine — fires having prevailed here to a dreadful extent about 10 or 11 years ago — but that only adds, if possible, to the extreme <u>romance</u> of the scenery — ~~just~~ 2 PM just partaken of a good Dinner — never enjoyed one more, but the sauce of <u>Hunger</u> perhaps gave it a richer <u>gout</u>[30] — eat part of a Fish caught by one of the Gentlemen on board with a trolling line — more Islands, larger than those we have already passed, but the very smallest of them covered with tall Pine Trees — the Mountains on the left begin to shelve more off from the Water — close to an Island of a conical shape, and at its base probably ½ of a mile in circumference — entirely covered with Brush Wood and here and there a few stumpy Trees — a pure solid Rock all round the part next to the water; it is called "12 mile Island" i.e. 12 miles from the end of the Lake — forward about 3 miles appears a very large and high mountain where Deer I am told are in great abundance but ~~which~~ which are almost safe from all human pursuit, in consequence of the place being so much infested with Rattle snakes, as to render a landing upon it quite dangerous — only one House seen since starting and that was sit^d· on Sabbath Day Point — the land too sterile for Inhabitants — but now signs of Cultivation begin more frequently to appear — on the <u>right,</u> numbers of small neat Farm Houses, with a few acres of clear land about them — new settlers I understand — but on the left nothing of the kind "nature madly wild appears."[31] Drawing towards the head of the Lake — 3 o'clock — Caldwell Point or Village, where we stop, in sight — from here the Mountains seem to form a complete Amphitheatre just round the landing place — the Lake however finishes about a mile further on — landed about 4 PM much pleased with the sail, and which by the bye was much enlivened by the merry Notes of a Key bugle,[32] played with much taste by one of the men — the finest Echo I ever heard — Lake George is about 31 miles long, upon an average breadth of ~~1½ miles~~ half a league — Caldwell Village is a small, but well built, neat place.[33]

Started with 3 others in a Hackney Coach for Saratoga Springs which we reached about 9 at night, having passed in our way a great number of small flourishing Villages, not however worthy of any particular praise on the score of cleanliness. Glenn's Falls rendered "elegiac" as forming the subject of a whole Chapter in the American Novel of "The last of the Mohicans" is about 8 miles from Caldwell Point — stopped there for near an hour. A person who has read the Work with any degree of attention might immediately recognize them — visited, & passed through the Cavern where the "<u>Ladies</u>" lay hid &c — our Guide a very well informed young man, and perfectly conversant with every thing relating to the place — at Saratoga put up at the United States Hotel, where there are now about 200 Boarders.[34]

Figure 1.1. "No. 24. Lake George and the village of Caldwell," Jacques Gérard Milbert, lithograph from *Itinéraire pittoresque du fleuve Hudson et des parties latérales de l'Amérique du Nord: d'après les dessins originaux pris sur les lieux* (Paris: Henri Gaugain et Cie, 1828). From the New York Public Library, Digital Collections. The village of Caldwell can just be seen in the middle left of this image.

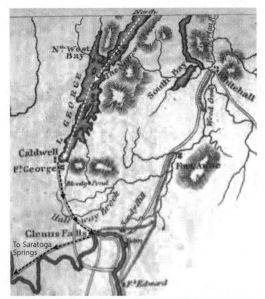

Map 1.4. Annotated map detail showing Scott's travel route down Lake George, landing at Caldwell Village (now the village of Lake George), then taking a stagecoach to Glens Falls, and from there on to Saratoga Springs. The original is "Map 12, Caldwell Village, Glens Falls," from [Theodore Dwight], *The Northern Traveller: Containing the Routes to Niagara, Quebec, and The Springs, with Descriptions of the Principal Scenes, and Useful Hints to Strangers* (New York: Wilder & Campbell, 1825). Courtesy of the New York State Library, Manuscripts and Special Collections.

Figure 1.2. "Glenns [*sic*] Falls," John Hill, etcher, after William Guy Wall, print no. 6 of The Hudson River Portfolio published by Henry J. Mergarey, 1822. Courtesy of the Metropolitan Museum of Art, The Edward W. C. Arnold Collection of New York Prints, Maps and Pictures, Bequest of Edward W. C. Arnold, 1954. The island in the middle of the river, where a figure in white can be just seen walking, is the location of "Cooper's Cave," which Scott visited as he passed through Glens Falls.

Figure 1.3. "No. 18. Saratoga Springs," Jacques Gérard Milbert, lithograph from *Itinéraire pittoresque du fleuve Hudson et des parties latérales de l'Amérique du Nord: d'après les dessins originaux pris sur les lieux* (Paris: Henri Gaugain et Cie, 1828). From the New York Public Library, Digital Collections. This view shows Saratoga Springs in the middle distance. A rapidly growing community, its natural springs attracted increasing numbers of visitors drawn by the reputed healing benefits of its waters. In 1826 Saratoga boasted ten hotels and boarding houses, one of which, the columned Congress Hotel, is prominently visible here. During his overnight stay, Scott stopped at the United States Hotel, another large, "first class" establishment centrally located in the village and not pictured in this image.

Wednesday, August 16th

Rose pretty early and went with a Mr. Phoenix[35] (a Fellow Traveller from St. Johns) to the spring and drank the Waters — (commonly called <u>Congress Water</u>) — they may be of "The Waters of life" but they have a most villainous taste, extremely saline, and strongly impregnated, as I am told with Carbonic acid — the Village itself is a very handsome place, although from the proximity of the woods it has quite the appearance of a place of Yesterday — a number of handsome well built Houses — the Hotels of which there are about a dozen, are generally fine large Buildings — started (by stage) for Schenectady — in passing stopt at the <u>Balston</u> [Ballston] Springs where there are no less than 4 or 5 different Kinds of Water — some of them the Same as the Saratoga Springs — am told that by frequent use, people even become fond of them — the most part of the Country hereabouts dull and uninteresting and signs of Cultivation very scarce — the Roads all the way from S. [Saratoga] very bad — nothing but a loose and pure Sand — and the least movement raises a cloud of it which renders travelling hereabouts very unpleasant — got into Schenectady about 1 PM.

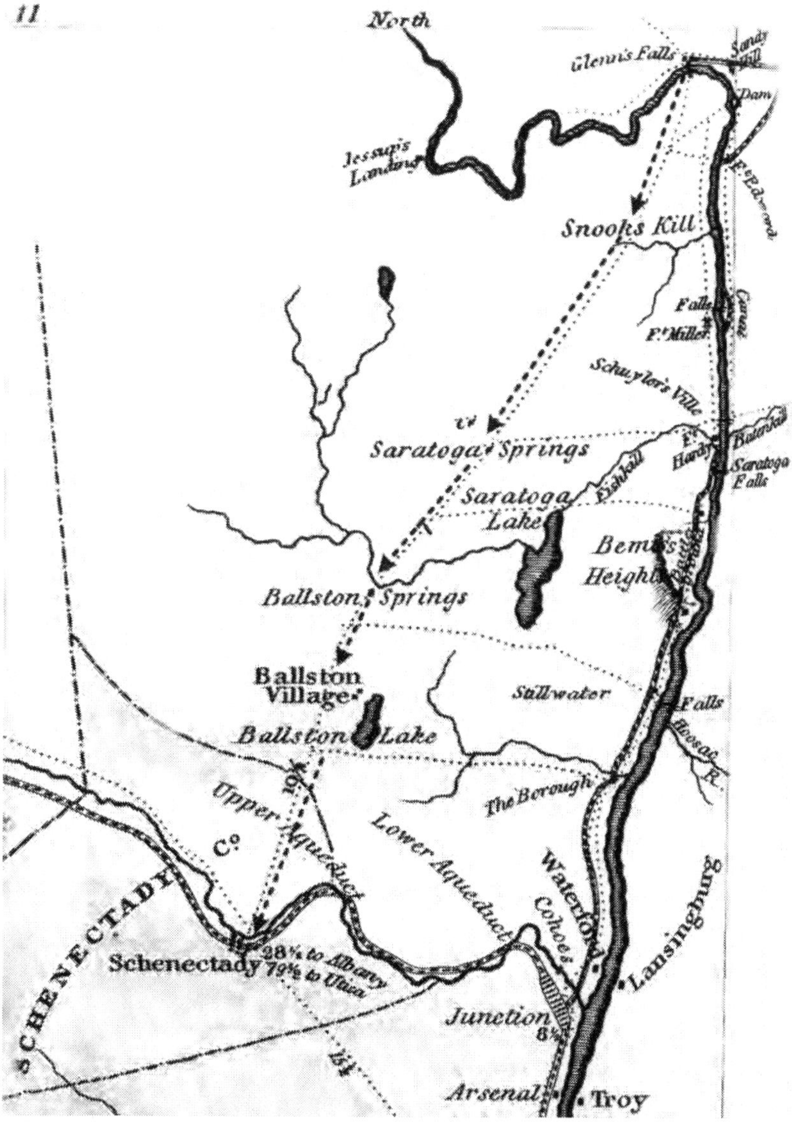

Map 1.5. Detail of annotated map showing Scott's travel route by stagecoach from Glens Falls through Saratoga Springs, where he stayed overnight. On August 16, 1826, he continued by stagecoach through Ballston Spa to Schenectady. The original is "Map 11, Glens Falls to Schenectady," from [Theodore Dwight], *The Northern Traveller: Containing the Routes to Niagara, Quebec, and The Springs, with Descriptions of the Principal Scenes, and Useful Hints to Strangers* (New York: Wilder & Campbell, 1825). Courtesy of the New York State Library, Manuscripts and Special Collections.

Chapter Two

"We were all immediately beset . . . by a set of Canal Boat Captains . . ."

Reaching Schenectady, the starting point for many packet boats carrying passengers westward on the newly completed Erie Canal, Scott takes a quick look around the city before boarding a packet boat bound for Utica. Once there, he continues this phase of his journey to Geneva, New York, by stagecoach.

Wednesday, August 16th (continued)

Got into Schenectady about 1 PM and we were all immediately beset (even before leaving the Carriage) by a set of Canal Boat Captains &c, setting forth the advantages of their several Boats, and with one voice beseeching our Patronage — the opposition very strong; abusive language, and sometimes Blows between the different owners and others interested, not at all uncommon I am told. After walking for half an hour about the town, which is a pretty large, but rather straggling place (a handsome College in it)[1] — embarked on board the Packet Boat Oneida in the Erie or Grand Western Canal, and am to be conveyed to Utica, a distance of 86 miles, and boarded, for one dollar! Cheap travelling surely — just what I want — find a most agreeable change in the steady and almost unfelt motion of the Boat, when compared with the rough & crowded stages — towed by 3 Horses and getting on at the rate of 4½ miles an hour — the accomodations [accommodations] on board not much inferior to the Steam Boats — the scenery fine, as the Canal for the most part hereabouts runs through high Land — was introduced to a Dr. Moore,[2] of New York, a fine, agreeable, well-informed man, & who immediately made me known to an American Presbyterian Minister (apparently a very young Man to be in orders) — eat a hearty supper and went to Bed a little after ten.

Thursday August 17th

All the Passengers warned to rise at 5 o'clock, no objections, although rather sleepy — the Cabin as hot as an oven — dressed and went on Deck — the Land through which we are now going being rather swampy gives the atmosphere the appearance of rain — got on shore and walked as far as the first Lock before Breakfast (about 2 miles), & at ½ past 7 took Breakfast, "good" — 8 AM at the place where we now are, the route of the Canal lies along the Bank of the Mohawk River — only about 50 feet above the R's [river's] level and merely divided from one another by the tow path — a strip of ground not more than 12 feet broad — 9 o'clock, arrived at the "Little Falls," very much worth seeing — got out of the Boat and walked up the Locks, of which from the sudden rise in the land there are 5 in about ½ of a mile — a very picturesque place really — immense piles of Rocks, as if produced and thrown into such strange confusion by some great convulsion of nature — walked up with Dr. Moore to the Village of Little Falls — prettily situated, and as neat a place as I have yet seen — the Canal here is supplied with water by an aqueduct carried across the Falls — a fine piece of workmanship — three stone arches about 60 feet high — the whole length of the Erection may be about 120 yards — the great number of Bridges across the Canal quite a nuisance to travellers — from their lowness, people are obliged to lie down flat on the Deck, (often not too clean) or get down below — got once knocked down by not observing one in sufficient time to take care — rec^d. [received] a severe blow, which stunned me a good deal — 4 PM arrived at last at Utica — apparently a very handsome little Town — upwards of 20 Canal Boats lying in the Basin here, & the hum of business pretty loud — went ashore with the Dr. and put up at Sheppard's Hotel a large elegant House[3] — walked out in a short time to see the place and certainly admire it much — wandered into the Court House where about 20 Students were undergoing examination to be rec^d. as Attornies — their appearance far from being prepossessing, and I observed that some of them had difficulty to answer the most simple practical questions — one young Gent^m. in particular shewed [showed] his free republican spirit by clapping his feet upon the Table close to which he sat during the proposition of the questions — could not but admire his sang froid.[4] Went to the Hotel to Tea, (in the same Room in which Lafayette dined when in U. [Utica])[5] and had the pleasure of being introduced by Dr. M. to a number of Gent^m. of high standing at the New York

Figure 2.1. "No. 1," 1825 unidentified watercolor sketch of a canal, which is probably the Erie, by John Hopkins Sr. Courtesy of the William L. Clements Library, University of Michigan, Hopkins Family Papers. In his 1825 journal of a trip he made across New York State, largely by the Erie Canal, Hopkins made a number of watercolor sketches. Although not specifying the precise location of every sketch he made, their context in his journal makes it likely that his unidentified canal sketches are of the Erie Canal.

Figure 2.2. "Erie Canal at Utica," watercolor drawing by unknown artist. *Our Travels, Statistical, Geographical, Mineorological, Geological, Historical, Political and Quizzical: A Knickerbocker Tour of New York, 1822.* [Attributed to Johnston Verplanck.] New York State Library call number 917.47 O93. Courtesy of the New York State Library, Manuscripts and Special Collections.

Bar now at this place in attendance upon the Supreme Court;[6] and among others to Mr. Emmet,[7] a B^r of the famed Emmet who was Executed as a <u>Rebel</u> during the troubles in Ireland and who himself was sentenced to Banishment — he is one of the most able professional Men in the State I understand, a pleasant & most gentlemanly character, conversed with him (particularly on the Laws of L. [Lower] Canada) for upwards of an hour — and derived much information from him respecting the powers &c of the different Courts in the U.S. — took a seat in one of the Western Stages for Geneva, a distance of 96 miles, & started at 10 PM (go night & day).

Friday, August 18th

Getting on in the stage, pretty good Roads, i.e. smooth enough, but so dusty withal that I can hardly distinguish the persons in the opposite seat — no rain the driver says for more than a month — not having been able to sleep all night I feel most miserably fatigued & regret I did not go by the Canal — breakfasted at Syracuse and stopped to dine at a place called Auburn where the State Prison is, a very handsome, large Building[8] — took up 2 more Passengers (and be d__d to them) the great Heat renders such crowded Carriages very unpleasant — about 2 PM passed <u>over</u> Cayuga Lake

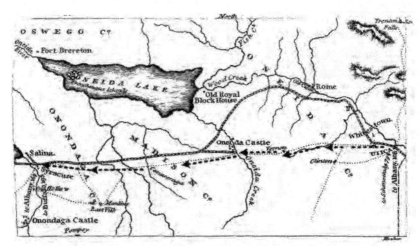

Map 2.1. Annotated map showing Scott's travel route by stagecoach from Utica through Syracuse, where he breakfasted on August 18, 1826, before the coach continued west to his destination, Geneva. The original is "Map 5, detail, Utica through Syracuse," from [Theodore Dwight], *The Northern Traveller: Containing the Routes to Niagara, Quebec, and The Springs, with Descriptions of the Principal Scenes, and Useful Hints to Strangers* (New York: Wilder & Campbell, 1825). Courtesy of the New York State Library, Manuscripts and Special Collections.

on a wooden Bridge thrown across, about 1¼ miles long. To me a singular sight — just as we cleared the Bridge, the opposition stage came in sight at the other end in full speed to catch us — a tight, well run race all the way to Geneva, where we arrived (about 7 minutes before the other) at ½ past 3 o'clock — put up at the Franklin Hotel — took a Bath, and went to Bed about 7, a good deal tired.

Figure 2.3. Etching, No. XL, "American Stage Coach," Captain Basil Hall, R.N., *Forty Etchings: From Sketches Made with the Camera Lucida, in North America, in 1827 and 1828 by Captain Basil Hall* (Edinburgh: Cadell & Co.; London: Simpkin & Marshall, and Moon, Boys & Graves, 1829). Courtesy of the New York State Library, Manuscripts and Special Collections. The stagecoaches used by Scott during his journey would have looked similar to this one.

Figure 2.4. Etching, No. VI, "Bridge Across Lake Cayuga," Captain Basil Hall, R.N., *Forty Etchings: From Sketches Made with the Camera Lucida, in North America, in 1827 and 1828 by Captain Basil Hall* (Edinburgh: Cadell & Co.; London: Simpkin & Marshall, and Moon, Boys & Graves, 1829). Courtesy of the New York State Library, Manuscripts and Special Collections. This dramatic image shows the bridge Scott describes as "a singular sight . . ."

Saturday, August 19th

Rose at 6 got my things all cleaned — breakfasted and about 9 waited on General Grieve[9] at his residence about a mile from the village, and delivered my Letter of Introduction — was rec[d.] with a most cordial welcome and treated with much politeness — invited to stop with him until tomorrow when he would drive me on in his own Waggon to Palmyra (21 miles off) — accepted his offer, got the loan of one of his Horses and went to look at the village — a beautiful place — Lake Seneca on the Banks of which Geneva is sit[d.] is 45 miles long upon an average breadth of 4½ — Returned to the Grange (the name of the General's estate) a fine and very valuable Property — dined, and about 5 PM went with him to see a Horse Race on the Banks of the Lake — some good running — had the honor of being introduced to a number of Yankee Gentlemen (very much like English Blackguards)[10] all Colonels, Majors & never lower than a Captain — went with a Mr. Hogarth[11] to bathe in the Lake and had a delightful swim, but when we came out of the Water found that all our Clothes had been conveyed away — a trick of Mr. Grieve's — Mr. H. had the <u>Brass</u>[12] to walk across the public Road to the Tavern where the General was to get them — and frightened all the People there — Mr. G. having previously given a hint when he saw him (H.) coming, that he was a Madman escaped from his Keepers, a general scramble to get out of the House — got home about 10 PM.

Chapter Three

"... was not at all Known by my Sister ..."

Twelve days after leaving Quebec, Scott departs Geneva in the company of General Grieve, who offers to drive him the twenty-one miles to Palmyra, where Scott's oldest sister's family lives. Quickly immersed in his family's activities, Scott's journal entries offer glimpses of ordinary life in western New York.

Sunday, August 20th
Started after Breakfasted [breakfast] with Mr. G. for Palmyra — Roads very dusty and the heat dreadful — after passing through a very pretty, & well settled tract of country, arrived about 4 PM at Palmyra, and found my relations and Friends all well — had some difficulty to recognize the younger part of the Family — and was not at all Known by my Sister who first saw me, for some minutes — passed a pleasant evening talking over old affairs.[1]

Monday, August 21st
Walked round the Village with my Br. in Law M[r]. Batchelor, by whom I was introduced to a number of the most respectable Inhabitants. P. [Palmyra] is a fine little place but, as I have been told rather unhealthy — surrounded on all sides by Hills of a conical Figure — called with B. [Batchelor] in the afternoon on a M[r]. Hullet who lives about a mile from the Village. One of the Judges of this County (Wayne).[2] Spent a couple of hours very pleasantly, and brought home the Son (a fine young fellow) to Tea with us — went with in the evening with my two sisters to the

Theatre where I saw the "Mountaineer" and "Bombastes Furioso" most cruelly murdered.[3]

Tuesday, August 22nd

Begin to think of going as far as the Falls of Niagara, 112 miles further on, — but fear the expense. Dined today at St. John's Hotel with M[r.] Batchelor — a large company and bad fare — had a long talk with a person at the table, whom I at first took to be a Play Actor, but afterwards found out to be a Lawyer — in the course of conversation he told me he had no idea by what Laws L. [Lower] Canada is governed — several Gent[m.] of the long Robe[4] reside in the Village, and I have been made acquainted with the most of them — sat up late to night, all the family at home, we had a comfortable Crack,[5] and B. & I had a tiffy[6] of good whiskey Punch.

Wednesday, August 23rd

Rose late, and did not manage to get myself dressed before Mid-day — got the blue devils[7] — walked out for an hour in the afternoon — my time prevented from hanging heavy on my hands by the unceasing attention and Kindness of my Sisters and B[r.] in Law — a fine, handsome Family of Children,[8] and Batchelor himself a pleasant agreeable Fellow — went out again to the Theatre, having got a present of a Ticket.

Thursday, August 24th

Took a walk about the Village and along the Banks of the Canal — did not go out after dinner, but read during the afternoon — in the Evening accompanied Margaret and Ann to a Church or Chapel of the Episcopal persuasion, where we had simply an Evening Lecture — the Presbyterians muster the strongest in this State, and a narrow, ill minded, bigoted & illiberal race they are — Burns' Scotch Elder[9] does not near come up in reality with a Yankee one — there is a Presbyterian Church, a Methodist Chapel, and the Episcopalians for the present being but few in number use the School House, which answers very well — the latter are what may be called the most genteel sect.

Friday, August 25th

Walked out in the morning — ~~one thing~~ one thing worthy of remark in all the villages I have seen in this Country — the Inhabitants ~~at each~~ seem to imagine (and rightly too I think) that each place will sooner or later become of importance, and consequently lay them all out on a large scale — fine broad streets, & generally speaking, at least a few good looking Houses in them — the American Gentry fond of having small Plantations of Trees before their dwellings, gravel walks, &c — wrote a long Letter to my Father. Batchelor sent us all again Tickets to the Theatre, where we accordingly went & saw Geo. Barnwell acted.[10]

Saturday, August 26th
   Nothing particular, did not go out much all day — General Grieve arrived in the afternoon on a visit.

Sunday, August 27th
   Kept in the House till the afternoon when I went with Ann & the General to the Presbyterian Church — the services much the same as in the Kirk[11] of Scotland, particularly in one thing, we had a prayer about the same length as the sermon, and neither of the first order — The Revd. Jeremiah Stocking, (the Minister)[12] to judge from appearances, of about as much education as the generality of itinerant Methodist Parsons — the P. [Presbyterian] Church has been christened "The Brimstone Factory" and by that name I have often heard it spoken of — a number of Irishmen looking for employment were not long ago sent to the Revd. Gent^{m.} who was represented to them as a Manufacturer of that article, and in one want of hands! — started immediately after service with Mr. Grieve & Batchelor for Geneva, where we arrived about 8 o'clock at night.

Monday, August 28th
   Heavy & continued Rain, which is much wanted — cleared up about 4 PM when we all walked up to the Village — saw squire Hogarth who introduced me to a number of his acquaintances in Geneva — got a talking with one (Yankee) Gent^{m.} about the differences betwixt the Government of this Country, and that of Great Britain — and in 5 minutes was completely convinced of his ignorance of every kind of government, even that of this own tongue, when speaking of the King of Great Britain[13] — was silly enough to get vexed with him — the U.S. a good place to fix an unsteady Man in loyal principles; the rank abuse so liberally showered upon the head of all Kings (and more particularly on ours) is enough to disgust even a thorough bred Radical — returned home rather late, and the most part of us a little stewed![14]

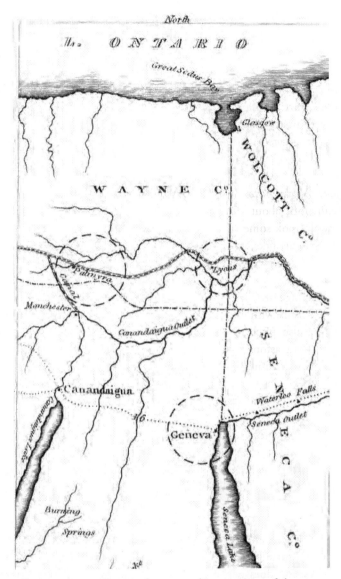

Map 3.1. Annotated map showing the geographic proximity of the communities of Geneva, Palmyra, and Lyons, each of which are mentioned in Scott's journal. The original is "Map 7, detail, Geneva, Palmyra and Lyons," from Theodore Dwight, *The Northern Traveller: Containing the Routes to Niagara, Quebec, and The Springs, with Descriptions of the Principal Scenes, and Useful Hints to Strangers* (New York: Wilder & Campbell, 1825). Courtesy of the New York State Library, Manuscripts and Special Collections.

Tuesday, August 29th

Started for Palmyra this morning with Mᵣ Batchelor by the round about way of Lyons (was not able to transact the business that took me to Geneva),[15] dined on the Road with a Friend of B's — arrived at Lyons about 3 PM where we stopped for about an hour — this is the County Town, went to see the Court House & Gaol,[16] both plain substantial Buildings — altogether a very pretty place — the Erie Canal runs through it — did not get into Palmyra before 9 at night, having again stopped on the way and took supper with a Gentᵐ, one of B's acquaintances — went to bed <u>instanter</u>.[17]

Wednesday, August 30th

Rain until about mid-day; eat some unripe plums, which made me quite unwell, took some medicine and felt so bad as to be obliged to go to Bed for the remainder of the day — don't recollect to have ever had such a severe and <u>sudden</u> fit of sickness — my sisters and two of the Children went out for a ride in the waggon with Bob in quality of Jehu[18] — in crossing a Bridge struck by another waggon, and the shock was so great as to throw Ann with little Stewart in her arms among the Horse's feet — Bob was also pitched out, and had a narrow escape from falling over the Bridge—but astonishing to say nobody was at all injured—Margᵗ and the other Boy (Erskine)[19] were in the back seat of the waggon & recᵈ no damage—if the Horse had moved, the wheels would have passed over Ann and the Child, & gone over Bob's legs.

Thursday, August 31st

Feel much better to day—almost well, but a good deal reduced by the severe vomiting—a delightful day—saw this morning a wooden House (30 by 40) removed from one part of the Village to another—rather a novel sight—done by Rollers, and only required about a dozen men—am told that even stone & brick Houses (when not <u>too</u> large) have been made to change places by the same means being employed—just thought of it, almost a month elapsed since I left Quebec, and really must confess that the prospect of hard work &c, does not at all tickle my Fancy, considering the pleasant time I have had of it. Went to meeting in the evening to hear Mᵣ Clarke.[20]

Friday, September 1st

Rose betimes[21] this morning and wrote to Gen. Grieve—went out in the evening with Batchelor & Peggy, and strolled for a couple of Hours on the Banks of the Canal—had a pleasant walk.

Saturday, September 2nd

Kept the House until evening, when I went with my B[r] in Law to a meeting of the Town Electors convened for the purpose of appointing Delegates to the Congressional & Senatorial Conventions to be held at a place called Newark[22]—expected to have heard some speechifying but was disappointed—had the honor of taking a <u>noggin</u> with the Meeting.[23]

Sunday, September 3rd

Went to the Episcopal Church both morning and afternoon with the Family—liked M[r] Clarke much better than heretofore, but he has a <u>Knack</u> of dwelling more upon the Justice & Judgements, than upon the mercy of God—very little difference betwixt the forms of the English and American Episcopalian Churches—the gaudy, vulgar dresses of the Girls, and what may be called the <u>Yankeeism</u> of the Men very striking to the eye of a stranger—observed more than one of the latter giving full employment to their pen knives in cutting, some their Nails, some chips of wood, and some the desks before them[24]—a Yankee is as bad as an Irishman, the moment he gets into a house, his hand moves almost mechanically to his pocket for the Knife. This evening I had the pleasure of reading Webster's discourse in commemoration of the late Adams & Jefferson—the language very fine and in every respect worthy of being called the Eulogy of such great, & such good Men.[25] <u>Mem.</u> [memorandum] to endeavor to procure a copy to take to Quebec with me.[26]

Figure 3.1. "The Nations Bulwark. A well disciplined militia," Edward Williams Clay, 1829. Library of Congress, Prints and Photographs Division. This satirical drawing of the Philadelphia, Pennsylvania, militia, visually dramatizes Scott's first-hand descriptions of New York State militia companies assembled for drill.

Monday, September 4th

Wandered about the Village to see the different Militia & volunteer Companies going through their exercises (this being the half yearly drill day)[27] strange names some of the <u>Corps</u> have, such as the "Slaughter House Rangers," the "Barefoots" &c,—the latter appellation is given to a Company from the great number of Privates without any sort of uniform, and several actually <u>barefooted</u>—a Drummer I observed, of the one of the most respectable & numerous Companies, <u>lacked</u> a Hat & Coat, & had his shirt sleeves tucked up to his shoulders—the Cavalry far, very far from having the appearance of "bold Dragoons" and the greater part of the Horses to judge from their unruly behavior "at the Roll of the Drum" seem to have been but little accustomed to the "Cannon's Roar"—a motley crew! Started in the afternoon with Batchelor for Geneva, and took <u>another</u> round about way—reached Vienna[28] just in time to see the different Companies <u>there</u> disbanded—much the same appearance as those at Palmyra—was introduced to a number of the officers—joined their Party and sat with them drinking and singing songs until midnight, when we all adjourned to the House of a Captain Hotchkiss,[29] where we ate some very fine melons—and afterwards got into Bed at the place where we put up, (<u>with a drop in our eye</u>!!!).[30]

Tuesday, September 5th

Rose at 8 AM not the least worse of last night's <u>spree</u>, and after eating a hearty Breakfast set off for Manchester[31] where we arrived about mid-day — a smart little village, about the same size as Vienna — got on to the Sulphur Springs (three miles further on), where we stopped for about an hour — the smell of the Water very strong, and felt a good way off[32] — both the smell and taste the very same as the spring at the end of the Suburbs at Quebec — beat a couple of Yankees — at the game of nine Pins![33] Passed through Orleans and some other small villages where my Bʳ in Law had some business to transact, and called on several of his acquaintances — did not get in to Geneva before 8 at night — went to the General's and found him rather unwell.

Wednesday, September 6th

Rose late, and spent the most part of the day up at the village with Mʳ Batchelor and his Friends.

Thursday, September 7th

Walked about the Farm with B. — went into the Woods, where we wandered about for an hour — lost a little Pocket Knife in my Ramble — set off for Palmyra, where we arrived about 9 at night. Eat a hearty supper, having just arrived in <u>Pudding time</u>.[34]

Chapter Four

"... I crawled back immediately with a cold sweat all over me ..."

Acting on his inclination to extend his journey further west to Niagara Falls, Scott departs Palmyra, traveling through Rochester to Lewiston. Once at the famous falls, he immerses himself figuratively and literally in exploring its varied natural features.

Friday, September 8th

Packed up a few necessaries, and about 2 PM started in the stage upon my proposed trip to the Falls of Niagara — reached Rochester at Sundown, where we stop for the night — put up at the Eagle Hotel, kept by one Ainsworth.[1] The Country to the West is not so thickly inhabited, consequently cultivation is not so forward as in the more Eastern part of N.Y. State — Rochester is a Town a little larger than Utica but wants the general neat, clean appearance of the latter place — the Episcopal Church is a very handsome small stone Building in the Gothic style of architecture, (a most favorite order in this country), the Tower or Steeple has a fine effect when compared with the tall & airy spire of the Presbyterian Church which stands close to it — a good looking Court House and Gaol, but what most particularly draws a Stranger's attention is the Acqueduct [aqueduct] — a large cut-stone erection, with 11 arches, passing over a pretty broad, and in some places Rapid River[2] — Boats can be seen passing <u>down</u> the ~~stream~~ under stream, and the Canal Boats, towed by Horses, <u>across</u> the upper one — perhaps the whole length of the acqueduct may be about 260 yards — walked about the Town — visited a saw Mill, calculated for cutting stone of which I saw a large Block ~~of stone~~ cut into 4 pieces while I was there[3] — took supper, and went to Bed at 9 o'clock as the stage starts early in the morning.

Figure 4.1. "Aqueduct Bridge at Rochester," detail, James Eights, 1823, pencil, ink, and wash, 3¾ in. high x 6 in. wide. Albany Institute of History & Art, gift of James Eights, 1836.1.3.

Figure 4.2. "No. 7, Genesee falls at Rochester, November 1825," watercolor sketch by John Hopkins Sr. Courtesy of the William L. Clements Library, University of Michigan, Hopkins Family Papers.

Saturday, September 9th

Left Rochester this morning about 5 o'clock; took a seat with the Driver outside, which I kept the most part of the day — tipped him a shilling, and he allowed me to act as Jehu for 2 or 3 miles, (4 horses) on the Ridge Road[4] — the R. R. [Ridge Road] worthy of observation, being for the most of the way to Lewiston an actual natural <u>Ridge</u> of Ground in some places from 40 to 50 feet high — doubtless at one time the boundary of Lake Ontario, as the Land all the way to the Lake is I am told almost a continued Flat — ~~passed a great number of small Villages~~ this is one of the best Roads the Driver says that he has ever seen, and he is all the way from the Tenessee [Tennessee] Country — by far the best <u>I</u> have seen in this state, and it is naturally so hard as to require but little, or no repair. Passed a great number of fast rising & improving Villages. When within about 30 miles of Niagara Falls the noise of the Cataract (the Wind being from that quarter) was quite distinctly heard, as well by myself as by all my Fellow Passengers, and I am told that when the Wind is fair, and immediately before Rain, the Sound can be distinguished even 50 M [miles] off — arrived at Lewiston about 8 PM where we put up for the night — eat a hearty supper, & treated myself with a <u>Highland</u> Dish — having Honey at the Table, I got some whiskey, and made myself some good <u>Athol</u> <u>Brose</u>.[5]

Sunday, September 10th

Cloudy Weather, and very much the appearance of Rain — wished to cross the Niagara River <u>here</u> into U. Canada [Upper Canada] and take the Road on that side to the Falls — but am told that a Carriage cannot be procured there at the present moment — the only stage having been lately broken down — sorry, as by that means am deprived of a close view of the fine Monument erected to the memory of General Brock on Queenstown Heights,[6] immediately opposite this place — close to the spot where he fell — it stands on the most prominent part of the Heights and from the top (to which access is had by a Cork-screw-stair-case) there must be a delightful view — it is about 160 feet high, and built of a pretty grey stone found at the place. The General and his two <u>aides-de-camp</u> now lie interred in a vault under the monument — got a good spy glass however and had a good sight of it — started with the same Party I came with from Rochester for the Falls — the weather having completely cleared up — stopped about 2 miles on this side of them to visit a place called "the Devils' Hole," and truly it is worthy of the appellation for it has a most

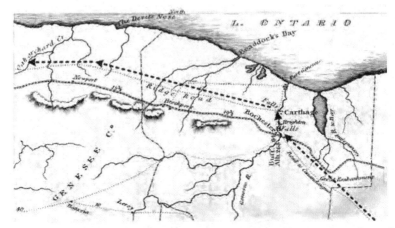

Map 4.1. Annotated map showing Scott's stagecoach travel route along the Ridge Road. The original is "Map 8, detail, Ridge Road from Rochester to Lewiston," from [Theodore Dwight], *The Northern Traveller: Containing the Routes to Niagara, Quebec, and The Springs, with Descriptions of the Principal Scenes, and Useful Hints to Strangers* (New York: Wilder & Campbell, 1825). Courtesy of the New York State Library, Manuscripts and Special Collections.

Figure 4.3. "Brock's Monument (From the American Side)," detail, William Bartlett print, 1838–1842. Although engraved twelve to sixteen years after Scott's visit, this print provides a visual appreciation of the prominence of Brock's Monument, a War of 1812 memorial located on the Canadian Queenston Heights and commemorating the heroic death of British General Sir Isaac Brook in that war. In his journal Scott records his disappointment in having to content himself with viewing the monument from across the river as shown in this view. Editor's personal collection.

hellish appearance, an immense pile of solid Rock — perhaps about 140 feet in perpendicular height over the River which runs close to its base — the whole body juts out from the Land, and is only connected with it by a mere strip — and it is the Holes or Caverns formed between the Rock and the main Land which is dignified with His Satannick [Satanic] Majesty's more familiar title — from the appearance of the banks of the River all the way from between Queenstown & Lewiston to the Falls, (a distance of 7 miles) the general opinion that they have worked themselves from that place (if not from Lake Ontario itself) is rendered not quite so hyperbolical — a glance of them caught every here and there, and the spray is seen rising high in the air — the roar getting louder every minute — arrived about 11 PM[7] at the Eagle Tavern[8] where we stopped — crossed over to Bath & Goat Islands, where we have a view of both Falls (a very extensive paper Mill, driven by Water on the latter),[9] but this is by a great deal the most unfavorable side for the view — it is even here however most awfully grand — wandered about the Islands which are connected with one another and with the American side by Bridges, over a dreadfully rapid part of the River — at one particular place at Goat Island there is a small flat Rock within about a foot & a half from the Edge of the precipice over which the Water tumbles — I was alone, and seeing by the marks of Footsteps that it was customary to go upon it, I got there, and kneeling down — washed my hands & Face!

> Alone o'er Floods & foaming Falls to lean,
> This is not solitude, 'tis but to hold
> Converse with Nature's charms, & view
> Her stores unroll'd (Byron)[10]

but I could not stand it long — "too much of a good thing is good for nothing," as the Proverb says[11] — after being upon the American side for 3 or 4 Hours, crossed over into U. Canada by a Ferry about 1/8 of a mile below the Great or, as it is more commonly called, the Horse Shoe Fall — in crossing completely drenched by the spray, which fell as thick as a heavy Rain about us — a number of most beautiful Rainbows formed by the thin rays of the sun falling upon it. The Ferry very troublesome for female Passengers, we had one on board who got alarmed — the Boat is small & for the greater security both oars are pulled by one Man, — we had to be landed twice on our way over, to enable the Boat with greater facility to get round several pieces of Rock (apparently fallen from above) which from

Figure 4.4. "The Devil's hole, on the road from Niagara to Lockport, State of N. York. Nov. 1825," watercolor sketch by John Hopkins Sr. Courtesy of the William L. Clements Library, University of Michigan, Hopkins Family Papers.

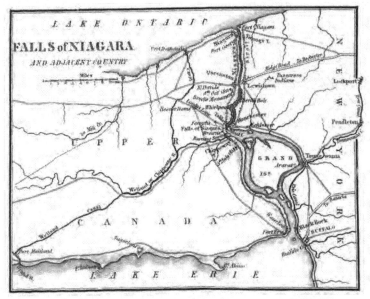

Map 4.2. Map, "Falls of Niagara and Adjacent Country," William Darby, *View of the United States: Historical, Geographical and Statistical* (Philadelphia: H. S. Tanner, 1828). Courtesy of the New York State Library, Manuscripts and Special Collections.

their situation occasion a particularly strong Current — just where we came over the River is about half a mile broad — landed, and took some time to reach the top. The ascent is accomplished partly by natural and partly by artificial steps — one of the Gentlemen with me killed a large copper coloured snake by a well directed blow with a stone, while it was just in the act of making a spring at him — it measured upwards of two feet in length — put up at the Pavillion, (kept by Wm. Forsyth)[12] sit[d.] close to the Chief Fall & from the Galleries of which an excellent view is had of all the surrounding scenery. Dinner being ordered we all walked down in the mean time to the Table Rock, to which we get by a flight of steps, & where I stopped about an hour — to attempt to describe my Feelings while at this spot would be impossible — the sublimity of the scene baffles all description!

> they gorge, & turn away & know not why
> Dazzl'd & drunk with beauty, 'til the heart
> Reels with its fullness (Byron)[13]

I lay down flat on the Rock, and put over my head to look below — when I had been there for a few minutes, one of the Gent[m.] behind, gave me a mere touch on the Back out of pure fun — I crawled back immediately with a cold sweat all over me, & for a short time felt quite sick at heart. I forgave the joke as he could not be sensible of what he made me suffer by his ill timed pleasantry — it was horror! — this is by far the best side for an advantageous view — in fact there is no comparison — from the Table Rock one cannot only see the Great Horse Shoe Fall, but also the one on the American side — (the latter is never viewed from any other better situation) — the Rock juts quite out from the main Land, and is split in a great number of places; some day or other not far off it will certainly give way all at once — large pieces which have already fallen off are seen lying below.[14] I introduced a wooden lath of about 15 feet in length, which I happened to pick up, into one of the cracks, & found no resistance as far as the stick could reach — the particular split I speak of extends about 30 feet, and upon an average is about ½ of an inch wide — dined about 5 PM & spent the Evening very pleasantly with a Gentleman just returned from Quebec, where he has been for some time — (a Mr. Brant).[15]

Monday, September 11th
Rose very early and again went down to the Fall to view the effects of the rays of the rising Sun upon the spray — most magnificent — breakfasted

Figure 4.5. "The Landing on the American Side (Falls of Niagara)," William Bartlett print, 1838–1842. Scott graphically describes his own climb up similar "artificial steps" on the Canadian side. Editor's personal collection.

Figure 4.6. "Niagara Falls," watercolor drawing by an unknown artist. *Our Travels, Statistical, Geographical, Mineorological, Geological, Historical, Political and Quizzical: A Knickerbocker Tour of New York, 1822.* [Attributed to Johnston Verplanck.] New York State Library call number 917.47 O93. Courtesy of the New York State Library, Manuscripts and Special Collections.

Figure 4.7. "Pavilion Hotel at Niagara," watercolor over pencil on paper, 1830, by James Pattison Cockburn, 1779–1847. With permission of the Royal Ontario Museum © ROM. Scott stayed here during his visit to the Canadian side of the falls.

about 8 o'clock, and about 9 waited on the Honorable Thomas Clarke[16] to whom I had an Introductory Letter from General Grieve, but had not the honor of seeing him, he having just left this place for the Village of Niagara (about 16 miles down) to hold the Court there — unlucky, as from the account Mr. G. gave me of the Gentleman, I had promised myself a great deal of useful information from his acquaintance — left my Letter however with a Card. About 11 AM went down with the intention of going under the Stream of Water formed by the Fall — rather a troublesome business for a person not accustomed to it but am determined to see everything about the Falls at all worthy of a stranger's observation — undressed to the Buff in a small House for the purpose close to the Table Rock, and put on a Canvas Shirt and pair of Trowsers [trousers] with a pair of light walking Shoes — got down to the Beach by a spiral stair case of about 140 steps and got from there close to where the water falls into the River below — (a perpendicular height of 150 feet).[17]

> Lo! Where it comes like an eternity,
> As if to sweep down all things in its track,
> Charming the eye with dread;
> Horribly beautiful! (Byron)[18]

NIAGARA, FROM BELOW,

Peter Maverick sc.

Figure 4.8. Artist's engraving of visitors (they can just be seen as dark figures on top of the rock at the right) under Niagara Falls at Table Rock. This is precisely where Scott descended and described the scene as "horribly beautiful." [Theodore Dwight], *The Northern Traveller: Containing the Routes to Niagara, Quebec, and The Springs, with Descriptions of the Principal Scenes, and Useful Hints to Strangers* (New York: Wilder & Campbell, 1825). Courtesy of the New York State Library, Manuscripts and Special Collections.

Proceeded on (under the conduct of a Guide) close to the Stream; as we begin to enter in under it, a sense of suffocation becomes most painfully acute, and the spray is so blinding that for the first 2 minutes I could not distinguish a step of my way — if it had not been for shame would have turned back — the noise of the Cataract is most awful, and I should think could not fail of inspiring with a reverential dread for the God of Nature even "the most desperately wicked" — we can only communicate our wishes to the Guide by signs, (he always holding you by the hand) who from being so often there can he says see with ease — however after having advanced 12 or 15 yards further in, I began to breathe more freely & again to have the perfect use of my eyes, as the water immediately above and for 40 yards or so further on falls over a smooth bed of rock, so of course is a pure unbroken body of water, without much of the spray — as white as chalk with foam, and as the eye gradually rises, turning into a beautiful green[19] — what a sight! "horribly beautiful" indeed!! The least slip of the foot here and we are irretrievably lost, nothing to prevent one from plunging right into the abyss ~~where~~ into which the water falls & which is not more than 20 yards down — the principal difficulties this length in, are, the want of air and the dangerous walking — the path way is upon the side of an ~~Kind~~ almost perpendicular rock, and the only way of getting on is by fastening the feet upon the out jutting parts of it, which from the continual moisture is by no means easy to do — I should think that the average distance betwixt the sheet of water, and the wall formed by the Rock over which it falls, (at least as far forward as one can see) is not more than 30 yards — it is hollowed out — I went as far in as the Guide told me was competent with safety (always acquiring courage by degrees) and then sat down to contemplate the awful scene before me — the Rock all around is ~~quite~~ green as grass, and as I have said extremely slippery & dangerous, particularly where climbing is required, which if you have the curiosity to go on as far as possible is often the case — perhaps the whole distance I went in under the great sheet was from 50 to 55 yards — there is one part of the Rock about half way in quite flat, where a number of names are engraved — the persons who took the trouble certainly must have had more patience than I pretend to possess. I remained under about 20 minutes — the greatest natural Curiosity I have ever seen or ever expect to witness. I took every possible advantage I could of the fine shower Bath which offered itself to me — but it has cost me more money than I expected for my trip — traveling is rendered dear about the Falls of N. not by the mere conveyances or Carriages, for they are as cheap here as in any part of the State — but by the numerous exactions for the use of Bridges, steps &c, — the people hereabouts are perfectly aware that Travellers would not for the sake of 2 or 3 dollars more lose the sight of any of the <u>unco's</u>[20] of the place, and accordingly act upon the principle of making Hay while the Sun shines — the charges for crossing Bridges, using stairs &c were never less than ⅓ Halifax currency,[21] and often half a dollar — if you complain, you have generally for answer that you need not use the conveniences unless you like but get down or across by any other way if you can &c — the mere going under the Fall cost me ¾ of a dollar — the Guide must have made this morning upwards of £5, but he says that sometimes for a week together not a person will go there — <u>he</u> certainly gains [earns] his money however, the mere going <u>to</u> the Fall so often not speaking of the injury his health must sustain by going so often <u>under it</u> (for he cannot take more than 2 at once) is worth the money — and he <u>is</u> often handsomely paid without going in by persons, who when they see the place they must pass, do not choose to run the risk — did not forget to take a good <u>Coo</u>[22] when I came out. On my way back to the Hotel I spent upwards of an hour alone on the Table Rock — in fact it is almost impossible (at least <u>I</u> felt it so) to withdraw the eye for a moment from what interests it so much — while sitting upon the Rock I saw several large trees launched over — they are often dashed to pieces before they can be again distinguished in the Water below — dined, and about an hour afterwards took my departure in a stage for Buffalo by the Canada Road, leaving with a sort of fond regret a place where I had received so much real pleasure and gratification — while I was at Forsyth's I amused myself looking over the the Register of Visitors names, where by the bye I put my own to let the world know I had honored the place with a visit — saw the following "Impromptu" as it was called written with a Pencil on the white Bark of a Tree close to the Fall, and dated during the year 1824 —

> (To N. Fall)
> Ye sport it bravely on my Soul,
> We sic' [word unclear, seek?] an arch to crown your Poll,[23]
>   But hark ye chap;
> The time shall come when a' will cease
> And e'en thy roaring be at peace,
>   In ruins lap.

appropriate enough I think, as far as I am able to judge — the Road we took lies all the way along the Bank of the Niagara River — this River varies in breadth from ½ to 6 miles — passed Grand Island, which half of which is purchased by the Jews for their new City of Refuge, to be under the immediate protection of the Government of the United States — Mr. Noah the Chief mover or he has styled himself "Grand Rabbi" is thought hereabouts to be <u>cracked</u> <u>in</u> <u>the</u> <u>upper</u> <u>story</u> — the Island is entirely covered with wood, and no signs of settlements have as yet begun to appear[24] — several Battle Grounds were pointed out to me, and I saw a number of the embankments thrown up by the British during the last War.

Chapter Five

"Had a narrow escape myself from sharing the same fate . . ."

Leaving Niagara Falls, Scott travels south by stagecoach to Buffalo, where he boards an east-bound canal packet boat. On this portion of his journey he passes through some of the Erie Canal's most famous landmarks, while enduring a mishap, before he arrives back at his brother-in-law's home in Palmyra in time for his sister Ann's wedding.

Monday, September 11th (continued)
Crossed the Ferry to Black Rock and although we are now upwards of 25 miles above the Falls, still the current is of a most astonishing Velocity — we were about three quarters of an hour in getting over although the River is hardly a mile broad at this spot.¹ Another Stage was all ready for us which we immediately occupied, and reached Buffalo about 9 at night, and put up at the Eagle Hotel² — a very extensive establishment; quite full — after a walk in the moonlight went to Bed, & slept sound enough.

Tuesday, September 12th
Got up about ½ past 5 in the morning, & walked out to view the Town — a very handsome place, and promises to become of importance in a short time — the <u>Emporium</u> of the <u>West</u> as it is often called — a fine & very elegant large Court House, a Bank, numbers of Churches, and

Figure 5.1. Etching, No. VII, "Buffalo on Lake Erie," Captain Basil Hall, R.N., *Forty Etchings: From Sketches Made with the Camera Lucida, in North America, in 1827 and 1828* (Edinburgh: Cadell & Co.; London: Simpkin & Marshall, and Moon, Boys & Graves, 1829). Courtesy of the New York State Library, Manuscripts and Special Collections. Note the canal packet boat in the left middle foreground.

Figure 5.2. "View Showing the Progress of the Work on the Lock Section," 1839, by Thomas Evershed. Although made thirteen years after Scott came through the flight of five locks at Lockport, New York, an experience he characterized as "the greatest artificial curiosity in this part of America . . . ," this view provides powerful visual testimony to the remarkable engineering feat accomplished there. Courtesy of the New York State Archives.

other public Buildings; and it must be remembered that all this place has been built since the year 1813 or '14 as about that time the then Town was burnt to the Ground by the British in retaliation of the burning of Newark & other villages by the Americans.[3] Breakfasted about 8 o'clock at a table where there were upwards of 100 persons, a good number of Ladies, some of them particularly handsome, but <u>fragile</u> looking, if I may be allowed the expression — <u>sensitive</u> <u>plants</u>. Embarked on board of the Canal Boat Utica[4] on my return to Palmyra — a good number of Passengers, amongst the rest a French Family, who travelled from the Falls with me, and to whom I was fortunate enough to be of some use as <u>Interpreter</u>, not one of them understanding a word of English — they are on their way from Paris to Louisiana — they appeared happy to find a person to whom they could speak; the Father is a fine old Fellow, a complete <u>François</u>[5] — in leaving Buffalo Creek we have a fine view of the Lake, Fort Erie, and the two Light Houses, (one on Each side)[6] — about 11 PM [it was actually AM] passed through Tonawanda Creek which is about 12 M. [miles] long, upon an average breadth of 60 yards — navigable for sloops all the way being never less than 12 feet deep — this creek lay very convenient to save a long Cut.[7] Getting near Lockport — for about 2½ miles before that place the Canal is cut through a <u>solid</u> <u>Rock</u>, and the whole of the cutting upon a stretch of upwards of 3 miles is never less than 30 feet deep — Lockport in itself is a plain looking little village, but is rendered famous by its Locks, of which there are 5 double ones upon the Canal, as close together as possible: as Niagara Falls are the greatest <u>natural</u> wonder, so Lockport, its Locks and the portion of the Canal adjacent, are considered to be the greatest <u>artificial</u> curiosity in this part of America[8] — the Locks & the <u>Cut</u> I speak of afforded employment to upwards of 1500 Men for three years[9] — immense quantities of very beautiful specimens of mineralogy, have been, & still continue to be dug up — the <u>petrifactions</u> are particularly worthy of observations; I purchased some of them, for which I paid pretty dear, and left besides in the shop an excellent pair of kid gloves, which cost me a dollar.[10] Sent back a note however by a Boat in passing to try & get them ~~back~~[11] — about 9 o'clock to night all the Passengers went ashore to visit Oak Orchard Falls, about 50 feet high, but at this Season of the year, very little water — the Canal is carried almost directly over them by an aqueduct of one arch — or more properly speaking a <u>Culvert</u> of ~~ab 50 feet or~~ 30 yards or thereabouts, in length — the place altogether had a fine appearance when viewed by the moon light.[12]

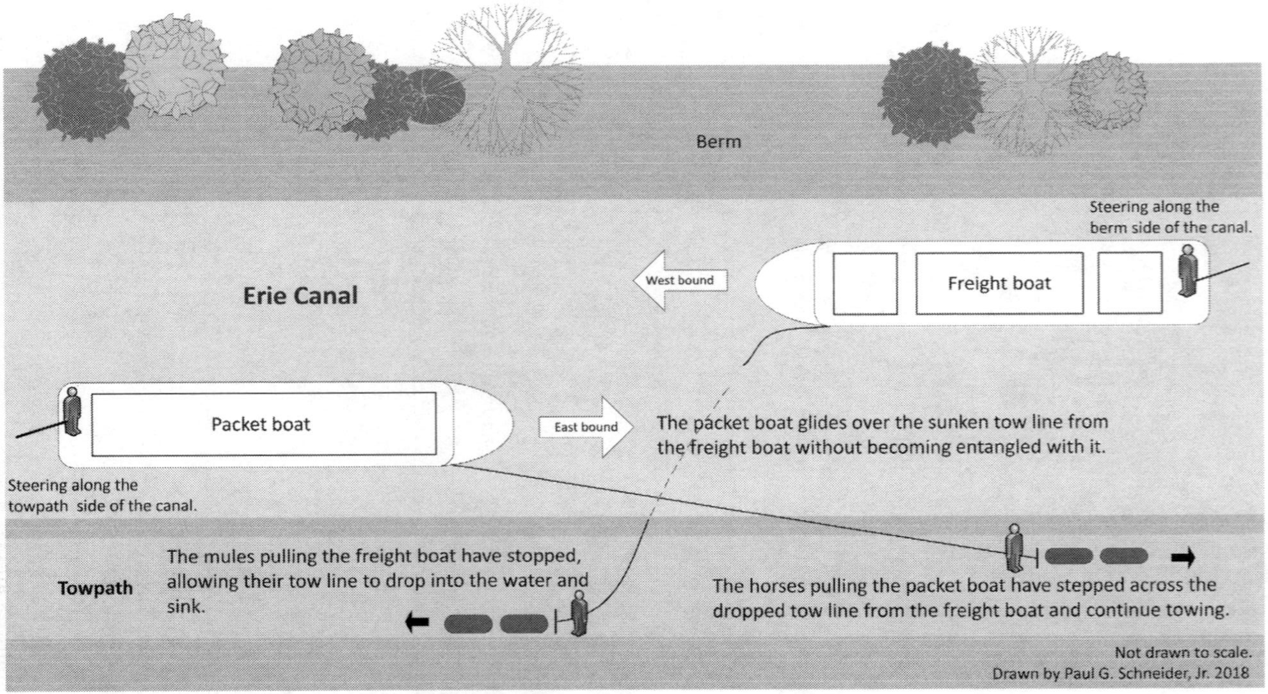
Berm
Erie Canal
Steering along the
berm side of the canal.
West bound
Freight boat
Packet boat
East bound
The packet boat glides over the sunken tow line from
the freight boat without becoming entangled with it.
Steering along the
towpath side of the canal.
Towpath
The mules pulling the freight boat have stopped,
allowing their tow line to drop into the water and
sink.
The horses pulling the packet boat have stepped across the
dropped tow line from the freight boat and continue towing.
Not drawn to scale.
Drawn by Paul G. Schneider, Jr. 2018

Figure 5.3. Schematic drawing illustrating the practical procedures taken by canal boat captains and drivers when passing one another. As passenger carriers, packet boats had the right-of-way regardless of the direction in which they were traveling. Otherwise, east-bound boats (which were headed to markets in Albany and New York City) had the right-of-way. Clearly, these operational practices were not followed properly, resulting in the accident Scott recounts in his September 13 journal entry. Drawn by Paul G. Schneider Jr.

Wednesday, September 13th

Up and dressed this morning by 5 o'clock, and for the most part of the day spent the time in reading. In passing another Boat coming up, a man sitting upon the Deck was unfortunately (by some mismanagement on the part of both Drivers) caught by the Tow Rope, which immediately whirled him up in the air, and dashed him down again with great force — the poor Fellow was most dreadfully bruised, and I do not believe will ever recover the injury he has received.[13] Had a narrow escape myself from sharing the same fate, as I was quite close to him when the accident happened — as usual an excellent dinner — cannot really understand how the Boats can carry Passengers at the low rate they do (3 cents a mile, including every thing) more especially when one considers the heavy Toll they pay to the State for the privilege of navigating the Canal[14] — reached Palmyra about dark, and found only Ann at home, all the rest of the Family having gone to Geneva. Wrote a Letter to M^r. Burroughs, at Quebec.[15]

Thursday, September 14th

Did not go out all day, amused myself with some Books, & at times <u>nursing</u> two of my Nephews (G. & E.)[16] who have caught an attack of a complaint very common in this State — the Fever & Ague.[17]

Friday, September 15th

This day I expected to be in Quebec, & I have not yet even left Palmyra! — <u>tempus fugit</u>[18] — had a most delightful walk with Ann about noon — fine weather, but rather coolish for the season — all the good Folks arrived tonight from Geneva, accompanied by General Grieve.

Saturday, September 16th

Nothing particular to observe.

Sunday, September 17th

Went to Church both morning and afternoon — dined at St. John's Hotel with a pretty large company — came home about 4 in the afternoon & about 5 the proposed marriage between Gen. Grieve & my Sister Ann took place[19] — the Ceremony is a very simple one & performed <u>by</u> (or rather in the presence of) a Magistrate — the whole of it did not take more than 5 minutes and simply consists of a mutual promise and engagement of the Parties towards one another to live as Husband and Wife, and thereupon they are declared to be so by the Magistrate, who by the bye, acts <u>merely</u> <u>as</u> a <u>witness</u>, and any other person of a proper age would do Equally well, only it has become customary always to prefer a Justice of the Peace to attend in preference to all others. No license or publication of Bans is required, and no Record or Register is ever kept — the Law of the Country is surely too lax on this point, but it is to be observed that in the State of New York and the greater part of the U.S. marriage is merely a <u>Civil</u> Contract.[20] After a long and very pleasant walk with some of the Palmyra Beauties came home & went to Bed.

Monday, September 18th

Did not go out till the afternoon, when I accompanied Peggy & Ann for a walk along the Banks of the Canal. Mʳ· Grieve left us for Geneva this morning — wrote a few Notes to several Gentᵐ· there, who had shown me some attention, bidding them good bye &c.

Tuesday, September 19th

Went in the Afternoon with both my sisters to Church, where the Bishop of the State (John Henry Hobart)[21] was to preach and administer the rite of confirmation — we had a most excellent discourse, from a very appropriate text, (i.e. our Saviour's Parable of the Invitation by a certain King, of Guests to the marriage supper of his son) — the Bishop is a man of plain, though very Engaging manners as a speaker — I thought his address to those who were confirmed one of the prettiest pieces of pulpit composition that I almost ever ~~had~~ heard — strolled out together all of us, probably for the last time while I am here.

Wednesday, September 20th

Busied myself for the greater part of to day in packing up my things and having ~~every~~ all in readiness, as I think of leaving this place tomorrow on my return to Quebec.

Thursday, September 21st

Another general training day here of both Horse and Foot — think that all the Drums in the County are collected in ~~before~~ this unfortunate Village, such a continued and wretched rattling I never heard — and they commonly stick pretty close to the same tune, (Yankee Doodle) — the Drum I observe is the most favorite part of Instrumental Music with the Americans, at least that part of them I have seen.

Chapter Six

". . . cannot help laughing at what happened in the course of the night."

On the evening of Thursday, September 21, Scott says good-bye to his sisters and nephews in Palmyra, and with his brother-in-law, William Batchelor, travels on the canal to Lyons. After a day trip to Sodus Bay with Batchelor to check on a possible job for Scott's brother, Bob, they return at night to Lyons where they part company. Scott boards a canal packet boat and undertakes the next stage of his return journey home via Syracuse, Utica, and Schenectady to Albany.

Thursday, September 21st (continued)
About 6 PM after rather a sorrowful parting, started by the Canal, with Mᴿ Batchelor who is to accompany me as far as Lyons — where we arrived about midnight — got on shore and took Beds in one of the Hotels there.

Friday, September 22nd
Propose to devote this day to go to Sodus Bay to see about the situation for my Br. Bob.[1] So after Breakfast, Batchelor and myself got a Gig, and started for the place, where, after passing through a very fine tract of Country, we arrived about mid-day; but was unfortunate enough to find the Gentleman I wanted to see (a Mᴿ Dolloway)[2] from home — the village of Sodus is sitᵈ on the Bank of a Bay stretching in about a mile from Lake Ontario — much gratified at the sight of the Lake — just the appearance of the Sea, more particularly as while we were there, a storm arose and the

waves ran pretty high — bathed in the water, and afterwards dined very heartily on Fish of which immense quantities I am informed are caught here — of all kinds — there is a handsome little light-house on the point of the Bay which I visited.[3] Got back to Lyons just in time to Tea — about 10 PM. M[r.] Batchelor took advantage of a Canal Boat going up, and left me upon his return home. A Packet going east passed about half an hour afterwards on board of which I immediately embarked, and am now once more fairly started on my Journey.

Saturday, September 23rd

Rose at 6 AM, and when I think of it, cannot help laughing at what happened in the course of the night. While in my Birth [berth] & asleep, I chanced to throw my arms about at a great rate (probably under the influence of some Dream). I awoke with my exertions, and found myself actually in the fact of hitting a Gent[m.] who was in the Bed next me, a slap on the Face, which he, apparently of a cholerick[4] [choleric] disposition & half asleep, took in high dudgeon,[5] & immediately showed fight — in his eagerness to resent the supposed injury he jumped up, & tumbled out of

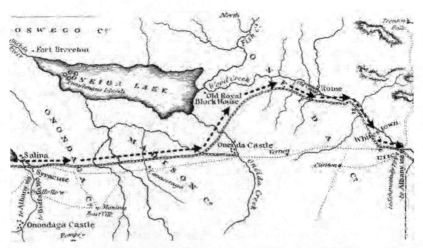

Map 6.1. Annotated map showing Scott's travel route on the Erie Canal from Lyons through Syracuse, Utica, and on to Schenectady. The original is "Map 5, detail, Utica through Syracuse," from [Theodore Dwight], *The Northern Traveller: Containing the Routes to Niagara, Quebec, and The Springs, with Descriptions of the Principal Scenes, and Useful Hints to Strangers* (New York: Wilder & Campbell, 1825). Courtesy of the New York State Library, Manuscripts and Special Collections.

Figure 6.1. "No. 5," 1825 unidentified watercolor sketch showing a packet boat in a lock probably on the Erie Canal by John Hopkins Sr. Courtesy of the William L. Clements Library, University of Michigan, Hopkins Family Papers.

Bed — overthrew a Chair and Basin of Water on the person under him in the lower Birth, who also it appeared did not intend to put up quietly with (as he imagined) such unprovoked usage — the <u>hula</u>-<u>bulloo</u> awakened all the other Passengers, very few of whom let the opportunity escape to grumble at their rest being broken — I was obliged to stuff the Bed clothes into my mouth to prevent my betraying myself by laughing, for to add to the joke, the Fellow himself who thought a good natured slap on the Face such a hard business, forgot what the matter was, said he was subject to walk in his sleep, and sneaked into Bed a good deal ashamed of himself — I could hardly avoid laughing in the Man's face every time I met him in the course of the day — the poor devil had his Nose a good deal scratched by his Fall. I have happened I see just to catch the same Boat which brought me from Buffalo to Palmyra — the Cap^tn. [captain] (Smith) is possessed of a great fund of information about the Country we are passing through & is of a very communicative disposition. Passed Syracuse about 4 in the afternoon, where I wished to have stopped for about an hour to examine the very extensive salt Works at a place called Salina, about 1 mile ~~east~~ north of Syracuse — but it rained hard — I could not depend upon another Packet passing tonight, and even if I staid till tomorrow (Sunday) could not see & visit them to advantage, so I made up my mind at once & just went on — the Works I speak of, cover very near ½ mile <u>square</u>, of ground. "The water from which the salt is made rises in the Marshes around the borders of the Village, or on the margin of Lake Onondaga, which is close by — Wells of 8 to 12 feet deep supply from 15, to 20,000 gallons a day, containing 16 to 25 ounces of Salt per gallon of Water"[6] — "O. Lake is a small collection of dirty water, not exceeding 6 miles in length & 2 in breadth," and as I have said "on its borders are the justly celebrated salines or salt springs, the largest & strongest in America," "in 1823 the Salt made in this County was 696,000 Bushels which yielded 87,000 Dollars to the Revenue of the State."[7] — At Syracuse I met with a M[r.] Wallace & his Lady,[8] formerly fellow <u>Travellers</u> of mine — we are now on what is called the Rome level, a stretch of ~~Land~~ Canal 70 miles long without a single Lock — went to Bed about 9 o'clock.

Sunday, September 24th

Arrived at Utica about ½ past 8 AM where after remaining for upwards of half an hour, proceeded on to Schenectady in the Canal Boat "Albany" — not more than a dozen Passengers & a very pleasant Party they are — I have scratched acquaintance with 2 young Yankee Girls on board — they appear to be rather above the Common run of American <u>Belles</u>, <u>mais</u> <u>vivent les Anglaises!</u>[9] Passed the Little Falls about 4 PM (see p. 20)[10] got ashore here with my new female acquaintances and walked with them down the Locks, a distance of about 2 miles I <u>guess</u>.

Monday, September 25th

Reached Schenectady (sometimes by <u>vulgarians</u> yclept[11] "Snackady") this morning about 9 o'clock — had a Letter of Introduction from Gen[l.] [General] Grieve to a M[r.] de Graff,[12] but which I could not deliver as we started almost <u>instanter</u>[13] in a Stage for Albany (distant by Land 16 miles, while by the Canal it is 31) where we arrived in about 3 hours — I put up at a large Brick Building situated in the most pleasant part of the whole City (near the Capitol) kept as a Boarding House by a M[r.] Cruttenden.[14]

Chapter Seven

". . . I have been I believe in every corner of the City . . ."

Upon his arrival in New York's capital city, Scott sets out to see as much as he can of its principal buildings and sights before heading north along the Hudson River the following day. He makes a visit to the federal arsenal at Watervliet, then crosses the river by ferry to Troy, where he stays overnight. Finding that the Court of Common Pleas is in session in Troy, Scott spends considerable time observing its judge and lawyers, vividly describing his impressions.

Monday, September 25th (continued)
    Albany is a very extensive & beautiful place. I am told it is about a mile square, and contains from 15,500 to 16,000 Inhabitants.[1] People from all parts of the Union are to be seen in it — the Grand Erie Canal finishes here by falling into the River Hudson upon the Banks of which R.[river], A.[Albany] is situated — the Basin found at the junction of the two Waters is a work of great magnitude, about a mile in length, by about one eighth in breadth and bounded all the way towards the River by a Quay 80 feet in breadth[2] — from 3[,000] to 4000 sloops & schooners & about 20 steam Boats navigate the Hudson[3] — visited the Academy a fine Building of free stone, with a spire[4] — I also went to see the Capitol — the rooms in which the Senate meet is much smaller than that in which the Representatives (answering to our H. [House] of Assembly) assemble — but both remarkably neat and tasty[5] — the State Library is also in this

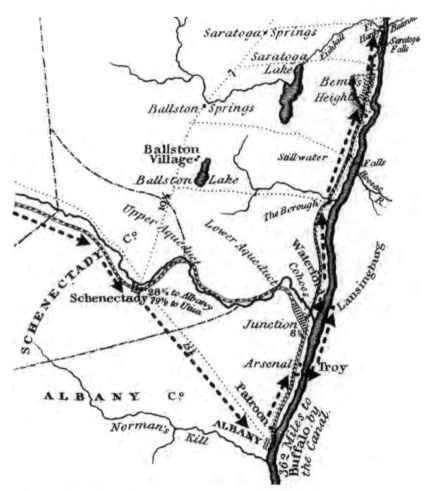

Map 7.1. Annotated map showing Scott's travel route from Albany to Troy, where he stayed overnight, taking a stagecoach the following morning north through Lansingburgh, Waterford, and then up along the Hudson River past the site of the Saratoga Battlefield. The original is "Map 11, Glens Falls to Schenectady," from [Theodore Dwight], *The Northern Traveller: Containing the Routes to Niagara, Quebec, and The Springs, with Descriptions of the Principal Scenes, and Useful Hints to Strangers* (New York: Wilder & Campbell, 1825). Courtesy of the New York State Library, Manuscripts and Special Collections.

Building, a small, but as far as I am able to judge a very choice collection of Books, & the Chamber is decorated with handsome Engravings on a large scale of all the first & most learned characters in the United States[6] — the view of the Country round from the Cupola[7] above is very grand — the Catskill Mountains (about 40 miles down the River) can be distinguished with the naked Eye. I have been I believe in every corner of the City, as M[r.] Cruttenden was kind enough to offer me a seat in his waggon on a (business) drive round the place & which I accepted — we were gone about a couple of hours — the general appearance of Albany is very prepossessing — the great number of Churches with their fine spires, & the other public Buildings give it a look of opulence equal to any place in the old Country I have seen of its size — State Street, which is the principal one is very capacious, — about 120 feet broad. DeWitt Clinton, the Governor, lives in North Pearl Street in a very plain looking House[8] — he is, generally speaking, a very popular Man, and I believe it is pretty well understood that he stands the best chance of filling the office of President of the U.S. at the next election — his principal opponent will be General Jackson — but I am told that J. is a mere soldier, and not fit for the place[9] — walked about until 7 PM when I took Tea, & at 11 o'clock went to Bed.

Tuesday, September 26th

Rose this morning sufficiently early to have a long & pleasant walk about the City before Breakfast, and at the same time I engaged a seat in the Stage for Troy, for which place we started at 10 AM and got there in about an hour and a half — the Road for the most part of the way lies along the Banks of the Hudson, and I enjoyed the drive very much — the Chief Arsenal of the U.S. is situated at Troy, and I was not a little surprised to hear that it hardly contained more than 50,000 stands of Arms. I went to see it — it is a handsome Building of Brick, covered with a kind of Roman Cement, and has altogether a fine appearance[10] — among other things I was shown some elegant pieces of brass Cannon — presents to the U.S. Gover[t.] [government] from the different powers of Europe on the final recognition of the Republic's Independence[11] — the River here is about ½ of a mile broad and divides the City into 2 parts, actually covered with Sloops & Schooners, and a number of Steam Boats — there are no less than nine regular Ferry Boats — fare across, 2 cents — we all put up at the Mechanic Hall, kept by a M[r.] Pierce, and apparently a good House.[12] I was pleased to learn that the Court of Common Pleas[13] is now sitting here,

Figure 7.1. "Congress Hall," detail, unknown artist, wood engraving on wove paper, 4¾ in. high x 8 in. wide. This imposing building, also variously known as Cruttenden's boarding house and hotel, is where Scott stayed during his brief visit to Albany, New York. Strategically located just across the street from the State Capitol, Congress Hall was popular with legislators and visitors to the city. Collection of the Albany Institute of History & Art, u1990.107.

Figure 7.2. Engraving of the New York State Capitol at Albany. New York State Library call number PRI 3855. Courtesy of the New York State Library, Manuscripts and Special Collections. When Scott visited the Capitol Building, he ascended to the cupola where he had a magnificent view of the city and surrounding countryside.

and accordingly was not long in finding out the Seat of Justice — to a person accustomed to the <u>dress</u> and mere outward show of a British Court, an American one has but a poor appearance — neither Judges nor Lawyers wear any Gowns, nor in fact any thing to distinguish them from other persons — not one in ten has a black Coat — the Chief Justice[14] had on a brown surtout,[15] white Trowsers [trousers], and a black silk Cravat, and was busily engaged in chewing Tobacco. I was about a couple of Hours in Court and from having heard several of the Gentlemen of the Bar open & close cases, address Juries &c, I cannot say I have formed any high idea of (their at least individual) Talent — very poor speakers. At Dinner I had the honor of being introduced to one of the Judges, and to several of the Advocates — (during session the most part of them who do not reside in the City put up at this House). In the afternoon I visited a Mountain[16] immediately behind Town from ~~wh~~ the top of which there is a very fine <u>landscape</u> view, and about a mile further on there is a very pretty cascade in a kind of rocky Dell — it is upwards of 50 feet high, and the sight of it well repaid me for the trouble I had in finding my way to it — by the

Figure 7.3. "No. 15. Falls of Mount Ida, above the town of Troy." Jacques Gérard Milbert, lithograph from *Itinéraire pittoresque du fleuve Hudson et des parties latérales de l'Amérique du Nord: d'après les dessins originaux pris sur les lieux* (Paris: Henri Gaugain et Cie, 1828). From the New York Public Library, Digital Collections.

time I got home it was time for Tea and I never enjoyed a Meal more in my life. Troy altogether is a handsome place, almost wholly laid out on right angles, and although not so <u>grand</u> as Albany, I think I would prefer it as a Residence, but the most part of the public Buildings are of Brick, and rather plain to please the eye of a stranger, and upon the whole I have spent a pleasant day in it, and am glad to have had the time to visit it — engaged a seat in the Coach which leaves tomorrow morning for Whitehall, where we arrive in time to meet the Lake Champlain Steam Boats.

Chapter Eight

"I have a very agreeable, pleasant Party with me . . ."

Boarding a north-bound stagecoach leaving Troy, Scott begins the next leg of his journey home. Along the way he meets two remarkable individuals, revels in the beauty of the passing scenery, and flirts with two pretty, young ladies. As he reenters his native land, he reflects on the country he has just left and the Americans he has met along the way.

Wednesday, September 27th

Started after Breakfast, proposing to sleep to night at Fort Ann, a distance of ten miles from Whitehall. I have a very agreeable, pleasant Party with me and I think that all along I have been peculiarly fortunate on that score — at a neat little village called Waterford, about 3 miles beyond Troy, we took up as a Passenger a General Von Schoonoven,[1] an elderly Gentleman, and certainly the most military looking character I have seen in the Country; a M[r.] Williams[2] one of my Fellow Passengers from Albany introduced me to him. I afterwards learned that he had been actively engaged during the whole of the last War, and he appears to be perfectly conversant with every occurrence at all interesting, either as it regards the <u>first</u> or the <u>last</u> War — the Country we are now passing through is completely <u>classic</u> <u>Ground</u> — it is the scene of a great many of the revolutionary struggles[3] — M[r.] Von S. pointed out to us, the Battle Ground of Bemis Heights[4] — the place where (a few days afterwards) General Burgoyne surrendered ~~surrendered~~ himself with his Army to the Americans under General Gates[5] — General Fraser's

Grave,[6] and a number of other remarkable places — passed through <u>lots</u> of villages, but none of them particularly handsome — arrived about 4 PM at Sandy Hill,[7] where we dined and stopped for about an hour — passed over a Bridge thrown across the North River[8] about ½ a mile long, and a short way further on, I see people engaged in erecting another at a place where it is nearly a mile broad — they are generally speaking, strong & substantial, & commonly roofed — the Road all the way from Sandy Hill is delightful and highly interesting — arrived at Fort Ann about 8 in the evening where I soon consoled myself with an excellent Supper — between Fort Edward & Fort Ann, a distance I should think of about 6 or 7 miles the State is now engaged in cutting a Canal from Grand, or <u>North</u> <u>River</u> to join the Grand Northern Canal (called a junction Branch) and which again empties into the famous Erie Canal, thereby making a clear Passage from the North River to the Atlantic, and also joining it more effectually with the waters of Champlain.[9]

Thursday, September 28th

Obliged much against my Will to rise this morning at 4 o'clock, and feel rather unwell not having been able to sleep all night in consequence of the Tea I drank at such a late hour — got into our stage again at 5 and

Figure 8.1. "No. 21. White Hall, Lake Champlain," Jacques Gérard Milbert, lithograph from *Itinéraire pittoresque du fleuve Hudson et des parties latérales de l'Amérique du Nord: d'après les dessins originaux pris sur les lieux* (Paris: Henri Gaugain et Cie, 1828). From the New York Public Library, Digital Collections.

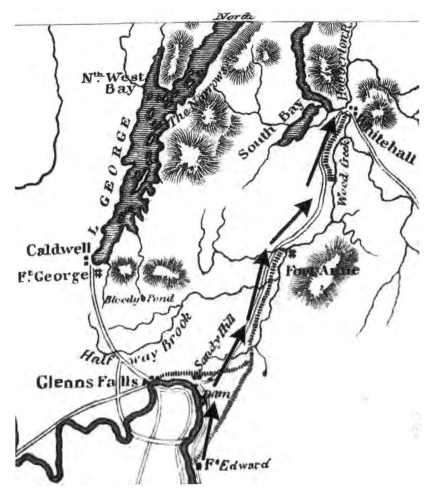

Map 8.1. Annotated map showing Scott's stagecoach travel route from Fort Edward to Fort Ann. Staying overnight, he proceeded the next morning to Whitehall, where he boarded the Lake Champlain steamboat *Congress*, the same boat on which he had first come down the lake. The original is "Map 12, Caldwell Village, Glens Falls," from [Theodore Dwight], *The Northern Traveller: Containing the Routes to Niagara, Quebec, and The Springs, with Descriptions of the Principal Scenes, and Useful Hints to Strangers*, (New York: Wilder & Campbell, 1825). Courtesy of the New York State Library, Manuscripts and Special Collections.

started for Whitehall, which place we reached about 7 and took Breakfast there — I am glad we came from Fort Ann with day light, as the Road all the way lies through a Country well worth seeing — natural scenery & curiosities in great plenty — rode down to the Steam Boat Congress,[10] on board of which I took a Birth for St. Johns L.C. There are upwards of 50 Cabin Passengers — Gen. Von. S. introduced me to a Mr Livingston one of the Judges of the Supreme Court at New Orleans[11] (all the way!) a most affable & pleasant Man, and who immediately, upon his being made aware that I was a Law student, turned the Conversation upon that subject — from his politeness I derived a good deal of useful Information — I learned from him, that in N. O. [New Orleans] a knowledge of the Spanish Language is a necessary qualification previous to an admission to the Bar. He seemed pleased at seeing any person from Canada ~~who had a capable of~~ related (however distantly) to his own Profession, and I was happy that my little Information about the powers &c. of the different Courts in Canada gave me an opportunity of enjoying more of his Conversation & Company than I otherwise might have done — I also had the pleasure of being made acquainted with two young Ladies who are going under the charge of the Mother of one of them as far as Burlington — I have heard much of the ignorance of the American Fair but really what few of them I have had the honor of being introduced to, give (at least as far as I can judge) no room for such an assertion. All the way from Whitehall to Fort Ticonderoga (22 miles) I was much gratified with the beautiful scenery — the Lake to the latter place, all the way down is extremely narrow, (in some places not above a stone cast) and so serpentine as to render it necessary in that short distance to stop the engine several times to get the Boat pushed round with poles &c — the "Fiddlers Elbow" in particular is worthy of a stranger's Notice[12] — All down below Fort T. [Ticonderoga] I have already seen in coming up (page 7, &c)[13] but, feel hardly the less pleasure in again passing through the Lake. By the bye I forgot to mention that yet two of the Men of War engaged in the Battle on that part of the Lake between Burlington & Plattsburg still lie not far from Whitehall — monuments of Yankee Prowess and British mismanagement — they are quite in ruins, or rather to speak more technically, perfect Wrecks — the one was the Essex, a vessel of 32 guns, ~~and~~ the name of the other I now forget — there are also the remains of a few Gun Boats.[14] On board of the Congress I have fallen in with a Dr. Anderson,[15] a fellow Countryman of mine, and now holding the situation of Professor of Materia Medica[16] in Vermont College — I find that he is a particular friend and old Ship Mate of Dr. Maguire,[17] an old Fellow Passenger with our Family from Halifax to Quebec; — that he has been trying for the last 3 years to find out Maguire — he was glad to profit by me going to Q. [Quebec] to write to his Friend. From the greater part of the Gentlemen I speak of I have received most cordial & Kind invitations to visit them if I ever again come near their places of abode. At Burlington, where we arrived about 9 PM almost the whole of the Passengers went ashore, and amongst others the two Ladies I speak of — I accompanied them to where found their Fathers were waiting for them, who gave me their addresses with a general invitation to their Houses — which I do not think (if ever I have an opportunity) I will be likely to neglect. I never in my Life saw Females whose company pleased me so much upon such a short acquaintance both of them quite accomplished, and certainly the most favorable specimen of the American Ladies I have ever seen, either as it regards personal or mental Beauties — passed Port Kent about 11 at night, after which I went to Bed to Endeavor to make up by a good Nap, the deficiency of last Night's Rest.

Friday, September 29th

Did not get up this morning before 7 o'clock, when we were just opposite the Isle aux Noix, & upon the whole I do not feel sorry at finding myself once more in His Majesty's Dominions, although to say the truth I will not soon, or easily forget the many pleasant days I have spent in the States. I freely confess that I went among the Americans a good deal prejudiced against them, and now that I am leaving the Country must say that the most part of those bad feelings are done away with. I now see the folly of forming any opinion of the People by the few whom a person has an opportunity of seeing and dealing with at Quebec, as (except the Visitors)[18] they are with but few exceptions, generally of the lowest and most ignorant class. From such Gentlemen, and Families whom I have had opportunities of being personally acquainted with, and introduced into, I have invariably received kind & friendly attentions, and been treated with much hospitality — there are without doubt not a few peculiarities in their manners which to a stranger are unpleasant, until one gets a little accustomed to them, but as soon as that is the Case they are hardly noticed or thought of. The Americans even yet, I may venture to say, are just in the <u>fever</u> of Republicanism, and some time must necessarily elapse before they can be completely <u>cooled</u> down to a <u>calm</u> consideration & enjoyment of all their many and inestimable privileges — the excellent & liberal system upon which all their schools & Seminaries of public Education are conducted will however, by Enlightening the minds of all classes, hasten this to be wished for <u>epocha</u>[19] — but yet "England, with all thy faults I love thee still"!

The Works[20] carrying on at the <u>Isle</u> <u>aux</u> <u>Noix</u> are immense surely — even in passing by, I see a great number of Men on the Shore engaged on them — the Ground I understand is not calculated for such heavy erections, being for the most part soft & marshy, and even already, part of the stone walls have sunk considerably — the utility (if any) of these terrible fortifications, have often been a matter of questions, but I never yet heard of a proper answer having been given to the Enquiry — the Water at the lower end of the Island is quite shallow, and in some parts the weeds rising from the bottom are seen in great profusion — the navigation hereabouts is very difficult and that alone would prove a sufficient safeguard I should think from any attack by Vessels — the Steam Boat touched several times before she got through — Breakfasted ~~about~~ at 8 o'clock and about 9 arrived at St. Johns[21] and was happy to find my Friends all well &c — did not go out much all day.[22]

Chapter Nine

". . . I really had no idea that such a small place could produce such a number of elegant Women . . ."

Back in Canada, Scott disembarks from the steamboat *Congress* in St. John's, where he rejoins his parents and sister. Through October into early November, he enjoys the company of his family and their circle of friends and acquaintances. He visits nearby military installations, attends dances, fishes, interviews a Revolutionary War veteran, and, despite complaining about the restricted social life of St. John's, clearly enjoys his visit before making his return to his home in the city of Quebec.

Saturday, September 30th

Went this morning to a Funeral or rather to attend, on the conveyance of the last remains of a M^r McNeil on board of the Steam Boat, to be conveyed to Vergennes for Internment. Called on a Mr Hallowell,[1] a Friend of my Brother James. After Dinner accompanied my Father on a call on a Mr Marchand,[2] a Friend of the Family — his House is situated about 2 miles from Town, and we had a fine walk, all the way along the Banks of the River — although St. Johns itself is but a <u>hum</u> <u>drum</u> sort of place, still the scenery round about is pretty Enough — Bellisle, Yamaska, & Scotch Mountains[3] stretching downwards upon the opposite shore have a fine appearance. On the top of the first, there is a small, deep Lake, in which I am told there is excellent fishing — the River for the most part of the way between St. Johns & Chambly, a distance of twelve miles, is

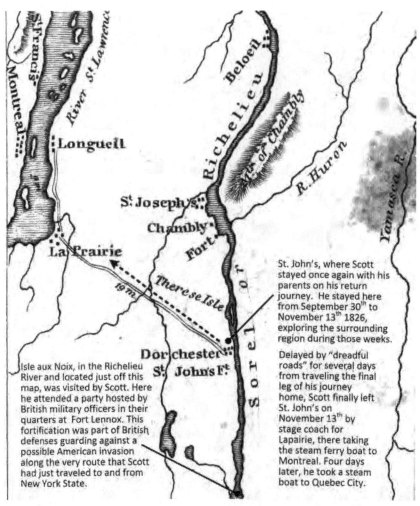

St. John's, where Scott stayed once again with his parents on his return journey. He stayed here from September 30th to November 13th 1826, exploring the surrounding region during those weeks.

Delayed by "dreadful roads" for several days from traveling the final leg of his journey home, Scott finally left St. John's on November 13th by stage coach for Lapairie, there taking the steam ferry boat to Montreal. Four days later, he took a steam boat to Quebec City.

Isle aux Noix, in the Richelieu River and located just off this map, was visited by Scott. Here he attended a party hosted by British military officers in their quarters at Fort Lennox. This fortification was part of British defenses guarding against a possible American invasion along the very route that Scott had just traveled to and from New York State.

Map 9.1. Annotated map of the region around St. John's, Canada. The original is "Map 15, detail, St. John's / Montreal, Canada," from [Theodore Dwight], *The Northern Traveller: Containing the Routes to Niagara, Quebec, and The Springs, with Descriptions of the Principal Scenes, and Useful Hints to Strangers* (New York: Wilder & Campbell, 1825). Courtesy of the New York State Library, Manuscripts and Special Collections.

not navigable, being full of Rapids, but a Canal fit for sloops, or as some say the clearance of the Bed of the River, betwixt those places I hear is in agitation — it is a pity that either the one or the other should not be carried into effect, as a clear navigation all the way from Quebec to the Hudson through Lake Champlain, would be the consequence.[4] M[r.] M. not at home, went into the House however and spent an hour very agreeably in the company of his <u>Cara Sposa</u> — a fine little woman.[5]

Sunday, October 1st

A cold, raw, uncomfortable day, and every now & then a drizzling shower of Rain — went to Church with my Father, and afterwards wandered down as far as the Phoenix[6] St. [steam] Bt. [boat] where we took a <u>Coo</u>[7] — stopt at home all the afternoon, the Weather cleared up a little towards evening, when I called with my Mother at the Parsonage, where we sat for an Hour.

Monday, October 2nd

Found amusement for the most part of the day in reading the American Novel of "The Last of the Mohicans" — the descriptive parts of the Work, particularly relative to Glenn's Falls, where I have been, (see back, p. 16)[8] ~~particularly~~ interested me a good deal — but Mr. Cooper's slavish imitation of the Author of Waverly's[9] style of writing is too perceptible to please, and not only in this but in the most part of his other productions — it says but little I think for his <u>independence</u> of <u>spirit</u>, at least on that point.[10] In the afternoon crossed the River with my Mother, where we stopped until Tea time — in the evening call at a Miss Heath's and took a hand at Whist[11] — played only <u>for Love</u>, but the greater part of the Ladies present being rather "stricken in years"[12] I did not feel <u>very</u> anxious about coming off a Gainer.[13]

Tuesday, October 3rd

Took a walk after Dinner with my Mother as far as the "Garrison" — this name is given to the old Fortifications of St. Johns, of which there are now little more than the remains[14] — about a dozen soldiers are still stationed here however, more for the sake of form than any thing else I expect. People are speaking however of Government's intending to rebuild the old Works:[15] a Bridge is about to be erected across the River and some opposition Steam Boats on Lake Champlain to run to this Port, will all no doubt tend much to the general improvement of the place — it is much wanted, and there is plenty of room for it — spent the evening with my Father at the Rev[d.] M[r.] Baldwyn's.

Figure 9.1. "The Barracks, St. John's C. E. (Saint-Jean, Quebec)," detail, unknown artist, 1846. Gift of J. Ross Robertson. Courtesy of Toronto Public Library, Toronto, Canada. When he visited this site on October 2, 1826, Scott wrote that "there are little more than the remains." He added, "People are speaking however of the Government's intending to rebuild the old works." This watercolor, showing the fort twenty years later, illustrates the extent of that rebuilding and attests to the continued importance of fortifications to the defense of British Canada against possible invasion from the United States.

Figure 9.2. "Custom House Square, Montreal, QC, 1830," watercolor by John Henry Walker, photograph, copied 1896. Used with permission. © McCord Museum, Montreal. Accession number: MP-0000.228.45. As a customs official stationed at St. John's, Quebec, Scott's father would have been familiar with this scene in Montreal.

Wednesday, October 4th

Did not go out until about 2 PM when my Father & I crossed the river & commenced gathering Mushrooms, they are very plentiful in this part of the Country, and we soon collected a good quantity — when we got home, found Mr. & Mrs. Baldwyn in the House — I went out to Miss Heath's[16] having been asked with my Mother to Tea, and the Parson stopped to spend the Evening with my Father — returned home about 10 o'clock.

Thursday, October 5th

Mr. Marchand, the Gentleman whom I called upon the other day, dropped in during the forenoon and sat for an hour with us — much pleased with him — Crossed the River, and ~~spent~~ wandered about on the other side for some time, came back to Tea, & spent the Evening with my Father at the house of one of his Friends, a Mr. Woods,[17] where we found quite "a snug whist Party."

Friday, October 6th

Nothing particular, — took a walk as far as the Garrison with my Mother, and ~~in the~~ after Tea called with Father on our Neighbour Dr. Morton,[18] an old acquaintance of mine at Quebec.

Saturday, October 7th

To day my Mother and I are left in the House together, as some business has called my Father suddenly to Montreal and my sister has not yet returned from St. Albans[19] (about 40 miles off) where she has been ever since I arrived. My Journal now a days, I cannot but observe is getting rather <u>prose</u>, for want of <u>material</u> — there is but little or no <u>food</u> for any thing of the kind in or about St. Johns — I intend keeping it going however until I am once more fairly settled in Quebec.

Sunday, October 8th

Went to Church in the morning with my Mother and took a long & pleasant walk with her in the afternoon on the other side of the River — brought home a quantity of excellent Mushrooms which we gathered there — they make fine Ketchup.[20]

Monday, October 9th

In the course of to-day's afternoon walked with Dr. Morton as far as a spring of Mineral Water situated in the Woods about 2 miles west of the

Village — drank of the Spring and found it by no means so unpleasant to the taste as I was led to believe it was — a kind of very distant resemblance to Epsom Salts, and when taken in a pretty large quantity has I am told much the same effect![21] — what I drank was not taken from the source, consequently it might be procured much stronger — it is situated upon private Property — our Minister M^r. Baldwyn called in and spent the most part of the evening with us — accepted of a seat in his Waggon in a drive which he proposed to make to-morrow to the Isle aux Noix.

Tuesday, October 10th

Started this morning about 7 o'clock — got to the Ferry to the Island at ½ past 9 and crossed over half an hour afterwards — called with M^r. B. on a number of Gentlemen, principally Military, and officers in the Gar-

Figure 9.3. "Officer's quarters, Fort Lennox, Isle aux Noix, Richelieu River, QC, 1892," photograph. Used with permission. © McCord Museum, Montreal. Accession number MP-0000.411.29. On October 10 Scott boats down the Richelieu River from St. John's to visit this fort and "its fine stone barracks." Here he attends a party in one of the officers' quarters. While this photograph dates long after Scott's 1826 visit, it gives a fine representation of the stone barracks he saw there.

rison of the Fort — dined with a M^r. Adams and received ~~from that Gm~~ at the same time an invitation from him to a large Party at his House in the Evening.[22] Spent the remainder of the afternoon in visiting the Fortifications of the place, in the company of M^r. A. and a number of Ladies to whom he introduced me — the Isle aux Noix is altogether ~~completely~~ flat — about 1½ miles long and at the broadest place ½ of a mile in width situated in the middle of the Richelieu or St. Johns River, [blank space] miles below Lake Champlain — the principal work is a large Moat, at the least 60 feet deep by 40 or 50 broad which can be easily filled with water from the River — there are a number of handsome draw Bridges erected over it, by which access is had to the fine Stone Barracks built inside — they are calculated to accommodate with ease 500 men, exclusive of officers — Hospitals &c.[23] Returned to M^r. A.'s about 7 where M^r. B. and myself dressed, and about 8 the Company had all arrived — I really had no idea that such a small place could produce such a number of elegant Women — about 30 Ladies and not more than a dozen Gentlemen, principally scarlet coated Gentry — played at Cards until about 11 PM when dancing began (plenty of Partners!) and kept up with great spirit until 2 in the morning — saw some of the Ladies home, and ret^d. to M^r. Adams' to sleep.

Wednesday, October 11th

Rose at 6 o'clock, and walked from the one end of the Island to the other, and with M^r. Baldwyn waited about 8 on a M^r. Wyatt[24] where we had been invited to break our Fast, and which I was not long in doing, much to my heart's content — as Miss Baldwyn (who I believe has been for some time here on a visit) goes home with her Father in the Waggon — I will be under the necessity I see of going home by the Steam Boat — The Phoenix passed about ½ past 10 and at 1 PM I was (<u>safely!</u>) landed at St. Johns — [four words crossed out and indecipherable] was most agreeably surprised to see my Sister, who had come home over night, and with whom & her Friend Miss B. I spent the most part of the Afternoon very pleasantly in walking about the Garrison.

Thursday, October 12th

Had not much inducement to go out to-day, so I managed to wear away the Forenoon in reading — after Dinner, I accompanied the Ladies in a walk by the River side, and returned just in time to Tea — M^r. B. called in the Evening.

Friday, October 13th

According to yesterday's arrangement M^r & Miss B. B. and myself started this morning about 10 o'clock on a fishing excursion — we procured the Garrison Boat, and got a couple of soldiers to pull — stopt out until after 2 PM having proved pretty successful. Mr B. is a very keen Fisherman, and as I myself am fond of the sport we managed to spend our time very pleasantly — in the evening we all adjourned to the Parsonage House, where we took Tea — & returned En bonne heure.[25]

Saturday, October 14th

Today Mr B. and myself again tryed [tried] our luck at fishing, and again [one word crossed out and indecipherable] proved successful — out about 4 Hours. and Spent the most part of the afternoon in walking about the large Common behind St. Johns — this Common I understand was once the scene of a pitched Battle during the Revolutionary War, and is now almost covered with a kind of earthen Mounds very much resembling Graves[26] — if I can manage it I will have some of them examined before I leave the place — My Father arrived to night pretty late from Montreal.

Sunday, October 15th

Went to Church in the morning with my Father and Betsy — and after service walked down to the Steam Boat Phoenix which had just arrived, on board of which I had the pleasure of meeting with Dr. Anderson (page 87)[27] on his way to Montreal, principally for the purpose of seeing Kean, who is again performing there.[28] I was pleased at seeing him in passing as I took the opportunity of introducing him by Letter to M^r O'Callaghan and my Brother James — a Mr Langdon, with whom he had made me acquainted called and spent the Evening with us — (Mr L. is Comptroller of the Customs at Burlington).[29]

Monday, October 16th

This morning after Breakfast I accompanied Mr Hollwell[30] of the Commissariat[31] in a cruise in his Boat — we had a fine stiff Breeze and I enjoyed myself well enough — spent an hour at his Quarters & borrowed a Flute & some Books from him — Miss B. called in the Evening noon afternoon & went with Betsy & me for a walk — during the Evening we played a Rubber of Whist.[32]

Tuesday, October 17th

A beautiful day — called again on M[r.] Hollwell (who introduced me to a Dr. Collis of the 76[th.]).[33] M[r.] H. & myself again went out in the Boat — tacked up the River upwards of 5 miles & came back that distance in 33 minutes — a complete Gale all the while we were out — in returning, boarded an Apple Boat and made the People in her pay toll in Fruit — stopt at home the remainder of the day, — saw Dr. Morton in the Evening at his Lodgings.

Wednesday, October 18th

My Father again gone to Montreal to be absent I believe for some days on Custom House Business — it now blows one of the most violent Gales (from the South) I have almost Ever seen in this Country — the River quite white with foam — in the Evening I walked down as far as the Beach and found the Water to have risen upwards of 9 feet since the morning.

Thursday, October 19th

Calm again — the Waters of the River completely subsided in a very short time — should not like to have been upon the Lake during the storm. Stopt at home until the Evening when I accompanied my Mother in a walk as far as the Garrison.

Friday, October 20th

Walked down to the Steam Boat before Breakfast where I again saw Dr. Anderson on his way home — this is his first visit I understand to Canada, and he seems to be much pleased with the Country, and the Inhabitants — after Dinner my Mother and I had a <u>Button Hunt</u> across the River, but proved unsuccessful.[34]

Saturday, October 21st

Nothing particular — did not go out all day.

Sunday, October 22nd

Went to Church with my Mother & Sister — had again the pleasure of seeing M[r.] Langdon from Burlington — he called in the Evening and staid [stayed] about an hour — a fine Fellow really — wished me much to go up the Lake with him and spend a few days at his place — a great hand for Mineralogy — his Collection of specimens I understand is very complete — shewed him the few I had brought with me from Lockport (p. 63).[35]

Monday, October 23rd

A rumor in Town this morning that Kean was here on his way to New York by the Steam Boat — went down to the Wharf to Endeavor to see the far famed <u>Roscius</u>,[36] but learned that it was all a <u>hoax</u>, & that he had made a further Engagement in Montreal — so I may have a chance of again seeing him <u>in his element</u> in passing to Quebec.

Tuesday, October 24th

Rain — cleared up towards the afternoon however when Bess & I called on Miss B. with whom we had a walk — called at Miss H.'s in the evening where I remained until 10 o'clock.

Wednesday, October 25th

To-day being fine Weather, Miss B. B. and myself took advantage of it to pay a long proposed visit to Mᵣ G. Marchand — found nobody at home — walked however as far as Mᵣ Baldwyn's Farm where we sat for an hour with the <u>Canucks</u>[37] who live there — saw an Habitant[38] (the Father of the Farmer) 83 years of age — the old Man has the full use of all his Faculties — fell into conversation with him when I learned that during his younger days he had been in the Military service and in the most part of the Engagements during the Revolutionary War — among others in the one on St. John's Commons in which the English with the assistance of the Guns of the Fort had the advantage — I have never seen this Battle mentioned in the History of the R. [Revolutionary] War, but the old Man nevertheless assured me there was one, and spoke of it also as being a long and very bloody one — he corroborated what I said about the <u>mounds</u> — he says they, (at least the greater part of them) are Graves, he says that he himself was one of the Burying Party, and that the dead were interred without any particular observance of order &c. He was in General Burgoyne's Army at the time of the surrender, and a Prisoner of War for upwards of 7 weeks — also in the previous Engagement with the Americans, when Fraser fell (p's 82 & 83)[39] — on our return to Town met Mᵣ M. going home.

Thursday, October 26th

Unpleasant Weather — did not go out much all day — Miss B. called in the afternoon and stopt for about an hour — in the Evening we had a regular Hail Storm, the first real appearance of the approach of Winter.

Friday, October 27th
    Went across the River in the afternoon with my Sister and walked about 3 miles down the Road — were gone more than 4 hours, — managed to spend our time very pleasantly.

Saturday, October 28th
    Rain all day, consequently did not go out — plenty of Books however.

Sunday, October 29th

No service in Church to-day — the Minister been at the Isle-aux-Noix since Friday, and prevented I suppose from returning by the bad Weather — called on M^r. Hollwell and returned him his Books — M^rs. & Miss B. came down during the afternoon; & my Father arrived in the Evening from Montreal.

Monday, October 30th
    Went down to the Wharf before Breakfast — an Irish Emigrant there got a quarrelling with another Man, and they at last came to Blows — in the heat of the Fight however, a schooner, on board of which the former had taken his passage for Whitehall, hauled out, and Pat[40] was in consequence obliged to get on board — he parted suddenly with the other to get into the Boat, and in going offered his hand to his opponent saying — "I'll see you again by Jasus before long, and in the mane time good-by t'ye." — I never saw any thing more characteristic of the Irishman — brave and generous — they shook hands cooly [coolly] enough at parting, mutually promising to fight it out the first opportunity — borrowed some of Mr Hollwell's books, (of which he has a small, but pretty good collection) and stopt at home the remainder of the day.

Tuesday, October 31st
    Took a long Stroll after Breakfast, <u>solus</u>[41] — a charming day — Hollwell called and invited me to a Card Party at his Quarters in the Evening — Went there about 7 PM (where Messrs. M.C. B. & W. soon arrived) and spent a few hours very pleasantly — came home about 12 PM.

Wednesday, November 1st
    Hard and continued Rain, no stirring out all day.

Thursday, November 2nd

Called at the Commissariat House in the course of the morning —
was introduced by M^r. H. to a Dr. Buckley[42] who has just come to Establish
himself in St. Johns — stopt at home all the afternoon — M^r. Baldwyn
popped in, in the course of the Evening.

Friday, November 3rd

<u>Rien</u> <u>de</u> <u>nouveau</u> — [43]

Saturday, November 4th

Did not go out until the Evening, when I took a walk alone — Dr.
Buckley and M^r. Hollwell called in the course of the day.

Sunday, November 5th

Went to Church in the morning with all the Family — had a pleasant
walk with them before Dinner — charming weather — spent the remainder of the day in reading — learned to night that sleighing had begun in
Quebec — high time I think to think seriously of getting home — have
no idea whatever of going down by Land!

Monday, November 6th

Went during the Forenoon to an auction of condemned Goods at
the Custom House — the articles generally speaking sold for their full
value — my Father purchased a few trifles — saw M^r. Hollwell & several
other Gentlemen of my acquaintance — from H. I received an invitation
to another Party at his House in the Evening — came on to Rain however
and I did not go out.

Tuesday, November 7th

Returned M^r. Hollwell his Flute &c — introduced by him to a M^r.
Miller, of the Commissariat Station at the Isle aux Noix[44] — took a Walk
on the St. Bt. Wharf, almost the only place where one can go, the Roads
are in such a dreadful state with the late Rains — called at the Parsonage
during the Evening.

Wednesday, November 8th

Engaged the most part of the day in packing up &c, proposing (if
possible) to start tomorrow on my return to Quebec, by the Stage.

Thursday, November 9th

Prevented from leaving to day for want of a Stage, and am told there will not be a public conveyance to Laprairie before Saturday morning — Miss B. called in the Evening and stopt to Tea — played a Rubber of Whist.

Friday, November 10th

Rain the greater part of the day, very little stirring out — Dr. Buckley called with some Letters for my Br. James in Montreal.

Saturday, November 11th

Again disappointed, no stage to day for Laprairie, as I am the only person in Town at present wishing to get there — no help for it. I see I must just wait patiently until Monday —

Sunday, November 12th

Went to Church with my Father in the morning — Have just been told that a Stage will certainly start to morrow Early for Laprairie of which I intend to take advantage, — called at the Stage House and Engaged a seat — Miss B. called during the afternoon — and in the Evening I accompanied my Mother to the Parsonage where we remained a couple of hours — learned much to my satisfaction that Mr B. proposes to visit Quebec next Summer when I hope to be able to pay a part of the debt of politeness I owe him. Considering what a small place St. Johns is, I certainly have contrived to spend my time very pleasantly in it. If the good folks here would just make themselves a little more sociable one with another, a very pleasant Society might be formed, but really there is more formality and etiquette in this miserable little village, than one might reasonably expect to see in a place thrice its size.

Monday, November 13th

Up this morning very Early — breakfasted about ½ past 7 thinking to start about 8 o'clock — but did not leave St. Johns before 11. Dreadful Roads — the horses walked almost the whole way to Laprairie where we did not arrive before 4 in the afternoon — only about 10 Minutes too late for the last trip of the Ferry Boat — she was still in sight when we got out of the stage — no other means of getting across, as the Wind is too high and cold to think of an open Batteau — put up at the Hotchkiss — took supper at 7 o'clock and tumbled into Bed a couple of hours afterwards, having

Figure 9.4. "The Place d'Armes, Montreal, QC, 1828," painting. Used with permission. © McCord Museum, Montreal. Accession number M385. This painting dates just two years after Scott's November 14, 1826, journal entry remarking on the progress of the construction of the "new French Church." This church, seen here at the left, rises above and behind the older church it replaced.

Figure 9.5. "Montreal General Hospital, Montreal, QC, about 1875," photograph. Used with permission. © McCord Museum, Montreal. Accession number MP-0000.3141. Here Scott visited his friend, Edmund B. O'Callaghan, who in 1826 supervised the day-to-day operation of the hospital. Although this photograph dates from the mid-1870s, Scott would have recognized the building.

spent the preceding part of the Evening pleasantly enough in rummaging over the shelves of what they were pleased to denominate "the Tavern Library."

Tuesday, November 14th

Up at 7 and started almost immediately by the Steam Ferry Boat for Montreal[45] — very cold indeed all the way over — fortunately for me I had borrowed a large traveling Cloak of my Father of which I experienced the full benefit — on my arrival in Town put up at M^r. Savage's in St. Paul Street, a private House[46] — and where I will feel myself comfortable Enough I think for a day or two — breakfasted with my B^r. James at Rosco's Hotel where he stops — purchased some things which my Mother wanted and sent them over by one of my Fellow Passengers who returns to St. Johns to day — called at M^rs. Goodman's[47] on Miss Jane B. to whom I had a Letter from her sister — une belle petite fille vraiment[48] — the new French Church much advanced since I last saw it — the workman now Engaged in putting on the Roof — a most superb Building — calculated to contain I understand when finished from [blank] to [blank] persons — the stile [style] of architecture is what may be called the Modern Gothic — spent the rest of the day with my Friend O'Callaghan where I dined &c.

Wednesday, November 15th

Did not go out until late in the day — called on my B^r. Harry and again on Miss B. at M^rs. G's from whom I got a regular Packet of Letters for Quebec — called on a Miss Hoyle, the sister of M^rs. Adams at the Isle aux Noix (by whom I was introduced to the Lady when at the Island with M^r. Baldwyn). I believe Dr. Leslie, a Quebec acquaintance of mine is very intimate in the Family[49] — received an invitation to the House for to morrow Evening — saw M^r. O'C. who had also been asked to meet me there — visited the Montreal General Hospital, — a very complete, and as far as I can understand, an excellently conducted Establishment, the Building itself is a very handsome one, and certainly contributes much to ornament that part of the Town where it is situated: in things of this nature Quebec is certainly far excelled by Montreal — part of the public spirit of the latter place would do the former no harm.

Thursday, November 16th

Went to James' office where I sat for an hour — called with him at M^r. M Cord's, where a M^r. Usher[50] (the B^r. of one of my Fellow Students at Quebec) is, and who also favored me with a Packet for Quebec — Called at O'Callaghan's after Dinner, and went together from his House to M^rs.

Hoyles[51] where we spent a very pleasant evening — introduced by Miss H. to her Family — quite agreeable People really — did not leave before ½ past 11 came home with O'C, at whose Lodgings I staid all night.

Friday, November 17th

After Breakfast walked down to Town, where the first thing I did was to take a Birth on board of the Steam Boat Swiftsure,[52] which leaves to night — called on a M[r.] Fry[53] one of my old Fellow Passengers on Lake Champlain — dined at 2 PM and at 3 called once more at M[rs.] H's (who

Figure 9.6. "Champlain Street below the Citadel, Quebec City, QC, 1865," photograph. Used with permission. © McCord Museum, Montreal. Accession number I-17502.1. In his journal entry for November 17, 1826, Scott, writing about the terrible state of the streets in Montreal, compares them with "our Champlain Street in Quebec . . ." He may merely have been making a comparison with a street immediately recognizable to his family, or it just may be possible that "our" Champlain Street is a more personal reference to the street on which he then lived in Quebec. This photograph, although taken thirty-nine years later, may provide a visual clue to the possible appearance of this street during his lifetime.

writes by me to Dr. Leslie at Quebec), and stopt there about an hour — saw O'C. in passing and came down to Savage's where I found Henry waiting for me, with whom after Tea I went to see James who is confined to the House with the Tooth-ache — sent my things on board of the Boat, and went down there myself, with Harry in tow, about 9 o'clock — the Streets are in a most terrible state with mud, and (from almost constant showers) have been so, ever since I arrived in Town — our Champlain Street in Quebec, although bad enough is not to be compared with them — started about ½ past 9 and at 11 PM cast anchor for the remainder of the night about 12 miles below Montreal.

Saturday, November 18th

Got under weigh (as I am told!) about 5 in the morning — a fine day but rather Cold — <u>Mem</u> [memorandum] — always to have a good Cloak if ever I go a travelling again (!) We have only two Passengers besides myself on board[54] — no quarreling for Births, like what I witnessed on board of the Chambly on my passage up; 3 months and a half ago — arrived at Sorel about 11 o'clock AM where we stopt for an hour — Went ashore there, called on Dr. Von Iffland about some business of my Father's but which I could not get transacted.[55] Walked about the Village — Sorel is a neat little place, and even now in the Fall of the Year, looks tempting to a person, who like me is fond of a Country life. Passed through the Lake and arrived at Three Rivers at 5 o'clock in the afternoon, where we remained until 8 in the Evening — some accident I hear has happened to the Engine. Called at Mʳ Fortier's[56] where I spent the most part of the time I was in Town — got on 24 miles more where we again cast anchor for the night at Batiscan[57] — a long passage this; and which is rendered the more dull by the want of Books or something else to help one to kill time: a small Library is a very desirable thing on board of these public Packets, in this respect we are far inferior to the Americans, who ~~and~~ even in their Canal Boats have generally got a pretty good collection of works of different natures for the use of the Passengers — for the reading of which they are commonly charged at the rate of a cent a volume, and often nothing at all. For those who are fond of Music I have seen some of the Canal Packets provided with a good Hand-Organ &c, out of which strains, (to tell the truth not at all times <u>seraphic</u>)[58] were <u>ground</u> by ~~the~~ <u>Boats</u>, at so much an Hour. Here, now, the Proprietors of the St. Lawrence Steam Boats seem to imagine that <u>Eating</u> ought to form our principal Enjoyment, and certainly they act up to their belief, if so it is, for such continual devouring will hardly be seen any where to so much perfection as on this River.[59]

Sunday, November 19th

Left Batiscan this morning at 6 o'clock, rose at 7 and went on Deck — a delightful clear day, but still rather cold — a good deal of Ice formed during the last 24 hours, and still augmenting very fast — large flakes seen floating about in all directions. The <u>sand</u> of my Journal is now nearly run out — the writing it has served now & then just to amuse me during an idle hour, and it was principally that motive which first of all induced me to begin it — if it has been sufficiently clear to give my Family, and those few Friends to whom I have ventured to show it, a general idea of the places I have seen or passed through, I will be satisfied, and feel pleased if it has been of the same service to them as it has to me, <u>i.e.</u> an auxiliary in killing time!!! when nothing better offered itself. I have been <u>several</u> places well worthy of observation, but hardly any more so than the River St. Lawrence and its surrounding scenery, although from having been so often up and down, its beauties to me are no such great matter of curiosity. At the upper part of Lake St. Peter (among the Islands)[60] and from Cap [Cape] Sauté all the way down to Quebec the scenery is particularly fine — the different bold Shores have a very striking and grand appearance, more especially when viewed from the Water, and the many romantic views round Quebec itself are a great treat to any person who is an admirer of the beauties of Nature. The <u>Sorel</u> River which falls into the St. Lawrence at the village of that name, up which I sailed two years ago, is really beautiful — the handsome villages built on its Banks, and the fine prospects seen from its various turnings actually charmed me — Belloeil Mountain[61] in particular, past the base of which the River takes its course, is well worth seeing. A prettier Country Residence than the Parish of Berthier immediately opposite Sorel could hardly be desired. I have been gone I see altogether upwards of three months and a half — I have staid away, almost through necessity, much longer than I at first intended, and although part (but only a <u>small</u> part) of that time may appear to have been <u>needlessly</u> spent, the pleasure my trip has yielded me, and my strong affection to "Home, sweet Home"![62] fully makes up for any loss I may have sustained or any inconvenience that may have arisen or might arise to me from my prolonged absence. Arrived at Hunt's Wharf, where I went ashore at ½ past 1 PM having been exactly 40 hours on our way down — I suppose the longest Passage made this Season.

(Finis.)

Afterword

Almost a month into his journey, Scott admitted in his journal entry dated August 31 that "the prospect of hard work . . . did not at all tickle my fancy." After serving as many as five years apprenticed to a commissioned lawyer, he was enjoying the independence and freedom associated with his trip through New York State. However, by the time he returned home in mid-November, he apparently was eager to once again embrace hard work. On December 11, 1826, just twenty-two days after disembarking at Hunt's Wharf in Quebec City, he was officially commissioned as a lawyer.[1]

It is not presently known with whom he studied law, but it is conceivable that it might have been with Joseph-Rémi Vallières de Saint-Réal, a brilliant lawyer, politician, and judge who trained young men for the law. After being elected Speaker of the Canadian House of Assembly in 1823, Vallières's own law practice increased, and in October 1827 he brought Scott into his firm as one of his partners. While their new association as legal partners has been characterized as "only moderately active," it represented a remarkably rapid rise for Scott.[2]

Vallières was a "moderate Quebec member of the nationalist Canadian party" (also known after 1826 as the "Patriotes"). One of the Patriotes' objectives was the political reform of British colonial governance of the country. Given his partnership with Vallières, it is likely that Scott shared his political views when he joined Vallières's legal practice.[3]

Scott's travel journal provides an oblique hint about his personal political stance when in response to his August 28 conversation with a "Yankee" gentleman in Geneva, New York, during which they compared the governments of the United States and Great Britain, he records that the man's "abuse" of the British king was "enough to disgust even a thorough bred Radical." Yet, whatever beliefs he held at age twenty-one—and he never uses his travel journal to articulate them—he clearly negotiated the political upheavals rocking Canada during this period, because from 1832 through 1842 he held the position of clerk of the peace and was "associated with the colony's upper legal circles."[4] In August 1842, he was appointed clerk of the Court of Appeals, a position he ably held until his death five years later.[5] During hearings conducted in May 1846 by the Select Committee of the Legislative Assembly, convened "to inquire into the state of the Judicial and Parliamentary Records in Lower Canada, . . ." Scott was praised for his attention to the records of the Court of Appeals, which were maintained in the courthouse at Quebec. That court's records were found to be in the "best order," Scott having "with a care and attention creditable to him, arranged all the papers belonging to it, made new indexes to them, causing also new binding to be made to the Registrars of his predecessors in office, without remuneration, and at some expense to himself."[6] Clearly, he had successfully navigated the shifting sands created by the political turmoil leading up to and through the armed Canadian Rebellion of 1837–1838 in Lower Canada.[7]

The positions Scott held in the Canadian court system suggest that his career advanced because of his legal training and knowledge—the pursuit of which is a recurring theme in his 1826 travel journal—and his organizational abilities as an administrator of judicial records. Unfortunately, his career was prematurely cut short by his death, and he never achieved a level of prominence that might have earned him an entry in the *Dictionary of Canadian Biography*.

Of his personal life, little is known beyond the bare facts of his marriage and death. On December 13, 1830, he wed Catherine Susan Fremont in Saint Andrew's Presbyterian Church in Quebec. Among those present at the ceremony and whose signatures as witnesses are decipherable were E. B. (Edmund Bailey) O'Callaghan, C. Fremont (brother of the bride), Josephine Fremont (sister of the bride), and Charlotte Noyer Fremont (mother of the bride).[8] Catherine was the daughter of Charles-Pierre Fremont. Her older brother, born in 1806 at Quebec, was Charles-Jacques Fremont, a prominent Quebec doctor, surgeon, and professor of medicine.[9] Scott's connection with the Fremont family through his marriage must have further solidified his position in the professional echelons of Quebec.

In 1831, the couple's first child, a daughter named Jane Charlotte Catherine Stewart Scott, was baptized in the Notre-Dame de Québec Basilica-Cathedral.[10] That other children were born through the years of their marriage is apparent; however, available genealogical information generated by contemporary descendants widely disagree with one another and are largely undocumented.[11] For example, none of the genealogies list a son, Alexander Stewart Scott, but a record of his burial on May 24, 1859, was discovered during research for this publication. The internment entry identifies the deceased as "the son of the late Stewart Scott [Scott often went by his middle name], Barrister at law, and of Catherine Fremont of Quebec." Sadly, this son, who would have been born sometime in October 1837, was twenty-one years and seven months old at the time of his death, almost precisely the same age of his father when he undertook his journey through New York State.[12]

Scott's own life, and that of his daughter Jane, ended with yet another cruel irony. As his travel journal illustrates, he avidly attended theater performances whenever and wherever he could. He was familiar enough with the plays being produced at the time to be critical of the performances he saw. Perhaps Jane shared his love of the theater for, together, on June 12, 1846, they joined the audience crowding the Théâtre Saint-Louis in Quebec to see an illuminated diorama created by painter and theater manager Mark Robert Harrison. This "major four-part work depicting Orléans cathedral, the enthronement of Charles X of France, and scenes from the Bible, prompted a Toronto critic in April 1846 to state that it far exceeded 'in beauty and effect any thing of the kind ever exhibited in Toronto.'"[13] Two months later, the show had reached Quebec. Scott and fifteen-year-old Jane must have been excited at the opportunity of seeing for themselves such an acclaimed display. Undoubtedly chatting about what they had just witnessed, the audience was beginning to make its way out of the theater at the end of Harrison's program when tragedy struck.

No better description of what happened next has been found than the following from J. M. Le Moine's *Quebec Past and Present: A History of Quebec, 1608–1876*:

> . . . when the audience were leaving the room, a camphine lamp suspended from the ceiling accidently fell and ignited the curtain in front of the stage. Instantly the place was in a blaze; and the theatre being crowded, in the rush which ensued to escape the flames, (the only mode of egress being through a narrow passage,) not less than forty-five to fifty human beings perished.[14]

Le Moine continues his detailed description of the deadly conflagration:

The blocking up of the theatre door was owing to the giving away of the stair case, leading to the boxes, under the weight of the crowd seeking an outlet; such was the pressure on the door, that no effort could force it in. . . . Those on the top of the living mass, by the falling in of the stairs became so firmly wedged in, that though in many cases their arms were free, they found it impossible to extricate their feet. Some friends entering through the windows, attempted by main force to remove Mr. A. Stewart Scott, and used such efforts as to wrench his shoulder out of joint, when anguish rang from the doomed man the exclamation "Leave me to my fate, Good by—Good by [sic]."[15]

With these last reported words, forty-one-year-old Alexander Stewart Scott's life ended along with that of his oldest child. To his family it had to have been a crushing blow. In the agony of a horrible death, Scott's last thoughts probably were for his daughter and his family. Yet his life did not end among the ashes of a theater fire, for so much of the essence of his young life survives today in the words he penned in his 1826 travel journal.

Appendix One

Toward the front of his bound journal, Scott devoted a single page to record the names and addresses of some of the people (and they are all men) he met during his journey. Certainly, this short list of ten names he wished to remember does not include everyone he encountered. While he does not articulate his reasons for noting them, it is possible that he viewed them as potential future business contacts or merely wished to remain in touch with them.

Not all the names listed here appear in Scott's journal entries, suggesting perhaps that he simply neglected to mention them by name at the time. In order to denote these individuals, their name is preceded by an asterisk.

When an individual's name is mentioned for the first time, either in a journal entry or here, what information—if any—discovered about that person is annotated in the notes.

Memoranda.

Mr. D. A. Phoenix
> 71 Front St. N. York.

Dr. Moore
> 48 Warren St. N. York.

Mr. Elisha Wallace
> Syracuse.

*Mr. Kenyon[1]
> Buffalo, on Lake Erie.

Professor Anderson, M.D.
> Troy (or Burlington College).

Gen[l.] Von Schoonoven
        Waterford, near Troy.

*D[r.] Sheldon[2]
        Sheldon, Franklin Co. Vermont

*M[r.] Barlow[3]
        Fairfield, Vermont.

M[r.] Langdon
        Compt[r.] of the Customs
           Burlington.

M[r.] Ezra Williams
        Russia Iron Works
           Clinton Co. N. Y.
           (10 miles from Port Kent on Lake Champlain)

Appendix Two

Scott kept a careful record of expenditures he made during his trip, the number of miles traveled, and the type of conveyances used. At the end of his journal, he entered these figures into hand-drawn tables: one for the trip going out to Buffalo, New York, the westernmost part of his journey, and one for his return to Quebec. The following is a facsimile of his accounts. On the last page, Scott summarized his expenses for the entire trip.

His expenses were recorded in Halifax currency, the official Canadian currency in use at that time. As reflected in Scott's accounts, Halifax currency paralleled the British units of pounds (£), shillings (s), and pence (d) but did not precisely equal its British counterpart. Calculating exchange rates among the multiplicity of currencies then in use both in Upper and Lower Canada, and in the various states of the United States, was challenging even to contemporaries of the early nineteenth century. Today, any attempt to accurately convert Scott's figures to present-day equivalents would be both problematic and misleading. No such attempt has been made here.

Fares, and Distances, Going

	Conveyance	Miles		Charges Hfx currency[1]		
From Quebec to Montreal	Steam Boat	180	£	1	5	0
Board &c. on board the Chambly			£		8	6
Expenses at Montreal				2	0	0
Montreal to Laprairie	Steam Boat	9			1	3
Laprairie to St. Johns	Stage	18			5	
Spent at St. Johns					2	6
St. Johns to Ticonderoga	Steam Boat	150		1	3	9
Expenses at Ticonderoga					2	6
From Ticonderoga to Lake George	Stage	3			2	6
Bottom of Lake G. to Caldwell Village	Steam Boat	30			10	
Spent on board of the Steam Boat					1	3
Caldwell Village to Saratoga Springs	Stage	27			10	
Expenses at the Springs					6	6
Saratoga Springs to Schenectady	Stage	30			7	6
At Schenectady					1	
Schenectady to Utica	Canal Packet	86	£		5	
Expenses at Utica					2	6

		Total, Miles	£		
From Utica to Geneva	Stage	96		15	
Expenses at Geneva				5	
From Geneva to Palmyra	Waggon	21		–	–
Spent at Palmyra				5	–
Back to Geneva	Waggon	21		–	–
Return to Palmyra (by way of Lyons)	Waggon	32		–	–
Again going & returning from G. to P. by way of the Sulphur Springs &c	Waggon	60		–	–
From Palmyra to Rochester	Stage	22		4	4½
Expenses at Rochester				2	6
From Rochester to Lewiston	Stage	80		16	3
Expenses at Lewiston				5	
From Lewiston to Niagara Falls	Stage & Ferry	7		2	6
Expenses at the Falls				11	10
From N. Falls to Buffalo on Lake Erie	Stage & Ferry	25		5	7½
Expenses at Buffalo				2	6
Total, Miles		**89Z**	**£**	**11**	**10**	**4**

1. Closely examining Scott's abbreviation here provided the clue to unraveling his meaning; the entry "Charges Hfx currency" means he sets down his expenses in Halifax currency, which at the time was the "official" Canadian currency. See "A Note from the Author: Money in Canada 1763–1858," in Robert C. Lee, *The Canada Company and the Huron Tract, 1826–1853: Personalities, Profits and Politics* (Toronto: Natural Heritage / Natural History, 2004), 12–13. See also James Powell, *A History of the Canadian Dollar* (Ottawa: Bank of Canada, 2005), 13–14, PDF e-book available at: http://www.bankofcanada.ca/wp-content/uploads/2010/07/dollar_book.pdf.

Fares and Distances
Returning

	Conveyance	Miles	£	Charges Hfx currency[1]	
From Buffalo to Palmyra (3 cents a mile)	Canal Packet	123		18	6
Spent at Palmyra				7	6
From Palmyra to Lyons	Canal Packet	16		–	–
From Lyons to Sodus Bay (on Lake Ontario)	Gig	15	⎱	4	
Return from Sodus Bay to Lyons	Do [ditto]	15	⎰		
Expenses at Lyons				3	
From Lyons to Utica (3 cents a mile)	Canal Packet	116		7	6
From Utica to Schenectady (Do)	Do	86		10	6
From Schenectady to Albany	Stage	16		3	
Expenses at Albany				8	
From Albany to Troy	Stage & Ferry	6		1	3
Expenses at Troy				7	
From Troy to Fort Ann &c.	Stage	70		18	3
Expenses at Fort Ann	Stage				
From Fort Ann to Whitehall				1	6
Expenses at Whitehall					

Description	Conveyance	Miles	£			
From Whitehall to St. Johns (L.C.)[1]	Steam Boat	165	£	1	10	0
Spent at St. Johns					5	
St. Johns to Isle aux Noix	Waggon & F[2]	12			–	–
Return from the Island to St. Johns	Steam Boat	12			5	
From St. Johns to Laprairie	Stage	18			5	
Expenses at Laprairie					3	6
From Laprairie to Montreal	Steam Boat	9				10
Expenses at Montreal					12	6
From Montreal to Quebec, &c.	Steam Boat	180		1	5	0
	Total Miles	**859**	**£**	**9**	**6**	**10**
	Going &c.	897	£	11	10	4
	Returning &c.	859		9	6	10
	Total, Miles	**1,756**	**£**	**20**	**17**	**2**

1. Lower Canada.
2. Ferry

Fares &c, Going ——— £ 6. 13. 9.
Do —— Returning 6. 15. 7. £ 13. 9. 4.
Board &c Going —— £ 4. 16. 7.
Do —— Returning 2. 11. 3. £ 7. 7. 10.

Total, £ 20. 17. 2.

Notes

Editor's Introduction

1. Information about the De Graff family can be found in Cuyler Reynolds, ed., *Hudson-Mohawk Genealogical and Family Memoirs*, vol. 4 (New York: Lewis Historical Publishing Company, 1911), 1574–1575.

2. George Rogers Howell and Jonathan Tenney, eds., *Bi-Centennial History of Albany: History of the County of Albany, N. Y., from 1609 to 1886* [. . .] (New York: W. W. Munsell & Co., 1886), 651–652.

3. Journal entry for Monday, September 25, 1826. The New York State Library was only eight years old when Scott visited. Created by legislation in the spring of 1818, it officially opened in 1819 with "669 volumes and nine maps on its shelves." Three years later, the collection had grown to "1,406 volumes and 369 pamphlets." Cecil R. Roseberry, *For the Government and People of This State: A History of The New York State Library* (Albany: The University of the State of New York, The State Education Department, The New York State Library, 1970), 5 and 7.

4. Ancestry.com, *Scotland, Select Births and Baptisms, 1564–1950* (database online) (Provo: Ancestry.com Operations, 2014), FHL Film Number 993425 (accessed June 18, 2018).

5. Ancestry.com, *Scotland, Select Marriages, 1561–1910* (database online) (Provo: Ancestry.com Operations, 2014), FHL File Number 1066757, 0103065, accessed June 18, 2018. Note: All genealogical information for Scott family members, except where specific primary sources are cited, is based on unsubstantiated but apparently mainly accurate information posted on the genealogical website Ancestry.com. See especially, George Scott family tree created by Patricia Lowndes Jennings at: http://person.ancestry.com/tree/78103455/person/40378835677/facts, accessed June 18, 2018.

6. *The Dundee Directory for 1809, Containing a Short Statistical Account of the Town: A List of the Merchants, Traders, &c. in Dundee and Suburbs, Alphabetically Arranged* (Dundee, Scotland: Coville & Son, 1809), 67. PDF e-book available at

"(1) 1809 [ID: 84955577], Scottish Post Office Directories," National Library of Scotland website, http://digital.nls.uk/directories/browse/pageturner.cfm?id=84955577, accessed June 18, 2018.

7. Unfortunately, while the British Parliament required ship captains of vessels carrying immigrants to North America to compile and file passenger lists at the port of departure, "few lists remain today so there are no comprehensive nominal lists of immigrants arriving in Canada before 1865." See "Immigrants Before 1865," last modified May 5, 2017, at the Library and Archives Canada website, http://www.bac-lac.gc.ca/eng/discover/immigration/immigration-records/immigrants-before-1865/Pages/introduction.aspx, accessed June 23, 2018. The approximate span of dates given for the Scott family's immigration to Canada is suggested by the fact that their youngest son, Robert F. Scott, was recorded as being born in Dundee, Scotland, on April 2, 1811, and that on May 11, 1818, George Scott, whose occupation is listed as tailor, signed a marriage bond in Halifax, Nova Scotia, Canada, for his eldest daughter, Margaret Jane Scott. For Robert's birth, see Ancestry. com, *Scotland, Select Births and Baptisms, 1564–1950* (database online) (Provo: Ancestry. com Operations, 2014), FHL Film Number 993425, accessed June 18, 2018. A digital image of the 1818 marriage bond is in the editor's possession, purchased from Nova Scotia, Canada, "Historical Vital Statistics," where it is recorded in Registration Year: 1818, Book 1800, Page 4143.

8. Journal entry dated Saturday, November 18, 1826. For Scott's passage on the Montreal to Quebec steamboat *New Swiftsure* and the number of steerage passengers, see Molson Coors Canada; Toronto, Ontario, Canada; St. Lawrence Steamboat Company Papers 1812–1892, MSS 475, vol. 29, *New Swiftsure* (April 25–November 21, 1826—Passengers, Freight and Fuel), accessed August 30, 2016, through Ancestry.com. The original is in Rare Books and Special Collections, McGill University Library, Montreal, Quebec.

9. Journal entry for Monday, October 2, 1826.

10. "Art. XII. *The Spy, a Tale of the Neutral Ground,*" *The North American Review* 15.36 (July 1822): 275.

11. The comparative literary merits of James Fenimore Cooper and Sir Walter Scott and their impacts on the American, Canadian, and British reading publics are far outside the scope of this work; however, their nationalistic themes are broadly addressed in Benjamin T. Spencer's *The Quest for Nationality: An American Literary Campaign* (Syracuse: Syracuse University Press, 1957). For Scott's influence, refer to pages 93–95; for Cooper's, see page 98.

12. George L. Parker, *The Beginnings of the Book Trade in Canada* (Toronto: University of Toronto Press, 1985), 12–13 (hereafter cited as Parker, *The Beginnings of the Book Trade*).

13. Parker, *The Beginnings of the Book Trade*, 16.

14. Parker, *The Beginnings of the Book Trade*, 25.

15. Journal entry for Saturday, November 18, 1826.

16. *Albany Argus & Daily City Gazette* (Albany, NY), Tuesday, September 26, 1826.

17. Journal entry for Sunday, September 4, 1826.

18. *Wayne Sentinel* (Palmyra, NY), Friday, August 25, 1826. The paper's masthead also reveals that Tucker & Gilbert, the bookstore's owners, were the newspaper's publishers.

19. *Lyons Advertiser* (Lyons, NY), Wednesday, September 20, 1826.

20. *Wayne Sentinel* (Palmyra, NY), Friday, August 18, 1826.

21. Parker, *The Beginnings of the Book Trade*, 15.

22. Parker, *The Beginnings of the Book Trade*, 14.

23. The titles of all but one of the plays he saw are found in his journal entries for the dates when he attended the theater, supplemented by short notes providing information on the playwrights and each play's full title.

24. For information on the Montreal theater, see Owen Klein, "The Opening of Montreal's Theatre Royal, 1825," *Theatre Research in Canada* 1.1 (Spring 1980): https://journals.lib.unb.ca/index.php/tric/article/view/7539/8598, accessed June 25, 2018. Scott's journal entry for August 7, 1826, indicates his presence in the theater's dress circle.

25. For information about Gilbert & Trowbridge's theater company, its announced appearance, and venue in Palmyra, see *the Wayne Sentinel* (Palmyra, NY), Friday, August 18, 1826.

26. Grimsted quoted in James Fisher, *Historical Dictionary of American Theater: Beginnings* (Lanham, MD: Rowman & Littlefield, 2015), 297 (hereafter cited as Fisher, *Historical Dictionary of American Theater*).

27. Glenn Hughes, *A History of the American Theatre, 1700–1950* (New York: Samuel French, 1951), 123.

28. Don B. Wilmeth and Christopher Bigsby, eds., *The Cambridge History of American Theater, Volume One: Beginnings to 1870* (Cambridge, UK: The Press Syndicate of the University of Cambridge, 1998), 143.

29. Quotation from Fisher, *Historical Dictionary of American Theater*, 247.

30. Located in Ontario County, Canandaigua was 208 miles west of Albany "on the great road to Niagara." Horatio Gates Spafford, *A Gazetteer of the State of New-York* [. . .] (Albany: H. C. Southwick, 1813), 151.

31. James D. Bemis to Mr. and Mrs. Daniel Ward, January 1804, transcribed and published in Madeleine B. Stern, "James D. Bemis: Country Printer," *New York History* 29.4 (October 1948): 404–405.

32. For a description of the Mohawk Valley, see George B. Cressey, "Land Forms," in *Geography of New York State*, ed. John H. Thompson (Syracuse: Syracuse University Press, 1966), 31 (hereafter cited as Thompson, *Geography*). For my reference to the concentration of settlements before 1800, refer to Katheryne Thomas Whittemore, "Buffalo," in Thompson, *Geography*, 410. For the origin of the term "the Great Warpath," refer to Eliot A. Cohen, *Conquered into Liberty: Two Centuries*

of Battles Along the Great Warpath That Made the American Way of War (New York: Free Press, 2011), 2.

33. Archer Butler Hulbert, *Pioneer Roads and Experiences of Travelers*, Historic Highways of America, vol. 12 (Cleveland: The Arthur H. Clark Company, 1904), 99 (hereafter cited as Hulbert, *Pioneer Roads*).

34. For a basic overview of the "New Military Tract," see Richard Schein, "New Military Tract," in *The Encyclopedia of New York State*, ed. Peter Eisenstadt and Laura-Eve Moss (Syracuse: Syracuse University Press, 2005), 1048. The role of private land developers and speculators in shaping western New York is the subject of William Wyckoff, *The Developer's Frontier: The Making of Western New York Landscape* (New Haven: Yale University Press, 1988).

35. Harold L. Nelson, "Military Roads for War and Peace—1791–1836," *Military Affairs* 19.1 (Spring 1955): especially 5–6.

36. Albert Gallatin, *Report of the Secretary of the Treasury, on the Subject of Public Roads and Canals; Made in Pursuance of a Resolution of Senate, of March 2, 1807* (Washington, DC: R. C. Weightman, 1808), 8.

37. For a brilliant discussion of this tension between union and confederation, see the first chapter, "In the Beginning," of Akhil Reed Amar, *America's Constitution: A Biography* (New York: Random House, 2005).

38. For the establishment of the Great Genesee Road, see Hulbert, *Pioneer Roads*, 99–100. For the Ridge Road, refer to Katheryne Thomas Whittemore, "Buffalo," in Thompson, *Geography*, 410.

39. D. W. Meinig, "Geography of Expansion, 1785–1855," in Thompson, *Geography*, 156.

40. Katheryne Thomas Whittemore, "Buffalo," in Thompson, *Geography*, 410.

41. Travis Bowman has written that Fulton and his partner, Robert R. Livingston, "named their new craft 'the steam-boat.' There was indeed no need for a fancier name since the boat was not only too small to be registered with the proper port authorities in New York, but was also the only working steamboat in America at the time. It operated for its first season as the steam-boat, although it was often referred to as the North River Steamboat or the North River." See "Bob's Folly Part 2: Making It Work," by Travis M. Bowman, June 24, 2011, blog entry on Clermont State Historic Site blog, at: http://clermontstatehistoricsite.blogspot.com/2011/06/bobs-folly-part-2-making-it-work.html, accessed July 5, 2018. He also has elaborated that "Fulton enlarged the boat in the winter of 1807–8 and officially registered it with New York State as the *North River Steamboat*. Fulton's biographer, Cadwallader Colden, changed the name of the vessel to the *Clermont*, and countless generations of schoolchildren have repeated the mistake." Travis M. Bowman et al., *Bob's Folly: Fulton, Livingston and The Steamboat* (Germantown, NY: Friends of Clermont State Historic Site, 2008), 60. See also both Russell P. Bellico, *Sails and Steam in the Mountains: A Maritime and Military History of Lake George and Lake Champlain*, rev. ed. (Fleischmanns, NY: Purple Mountain Press, 2001), 262

(hereafter cited as Bellico, *Sails and Steam in the Mountains*) and Len F. Tantillo, "Fulton's Steamboat at Clermont, 1807: A Glimpse into the Artist's Process," *Sea History* 163 (Summer 2018): 30.

42. Arthur G. Adams, "steamboats," in *The Encyclopedia of New York State*, ed. Peter Eisenstadt and Laura-Eve Moss (Syracuse: Syracuse University Press, 2005), 1476.

43. Bellico, *Sails and Steam in the Mountains*. For establishment of Lake Champlain steamboat service, see page 264. For the Lake George service, refer to page 300.

44. The definitive account of canal boats on Lake Champlain is Arthur B. Cohn, *Lake Champlain's Sailing Canal Boats: An Illustrated Journey from Burlington Bay to the Hudson River: Building the Canal Schooner Lois McClure* (Basin Harbor, VT: Lake Champlain Maritime Museum, 2003).

45. Carol Sheriff, *The Artificial River: The Erie Canal and the Paradox of Progress, 1817–1862* (New York: Hill and Wang, 1996), 52.

46. "New Line of Stages," *Album* (Rochester, NY), August 1, 1826.

47. *Albany Argus & Daily City Gazette* (Albany, NY), September 26, 1826.

48. Will Mackintosh, " 'Ticketed Through': The Commodification of Travel in the Nineteenth Century," *Journal of the Early Republic* 32.1 (Spring 2012): 65–66.

49. Richard H. Gassan, *The Birth of American Tourism: New York, the Hudson Valley, and American Culture, 1790–1830* (Amherst: University of Massachusetts Press, 2008), 2 (hereafter cited as Gassan, *American Tourism*).

50. For the comparison of the *Niles' Weekly Register* with the *New York Times* and Washington *Post* newspapers, see W. H. Earle, "Niles' Register, 1811–1849: Window on the World," Niles' Register: Cumulative Index, 1811–1849, website at: http://www.nilesregister.com/NRessay.htm, accessed July 3, 2018. For the article "Visitors of the North," refer to *Niles' Weekly Register* (Baltimore, MD), September 16, 1826, Internet Archive at https://archive.org/details/nilesweeklyregis3118balt (original from University of Florida), PDF.

51. Gassan, *American Tourism*, 71 and 73.

52. Theodore Dwight, *The Northern Traveller: Containing the Routes to Niagara, Quebec, and The Springs, with Descriptions of the Principal Scenes, and Useful Hints to Strangers* (New York: Wilder & Campbell, 1825), iii, HathiTrust Digital Library at: https://babel.hathitrust.org/cgi/pt?id=aeu.ark:/13960/t3611sd22;view=1up;seq=169 (original from University of Alberta), PDF (hereafter cited as Dwight, *Northern Traveller, 1825*).

53. For the accommodations on canal packet boats and the disparity of travelers' reactions, see Gassan, *American Tourism*, 98–100.

54. Dwight, *Northern Traveller, 1825*, iii.

55. Colonel William Leete Stone, "From New York to Niagara: Journal of a Tour, in Part by the Erie Canal, in the Year 1829," in *Buffalo Historical Society Publications*, vol. 14, ed. Frank H. Severance (Buffalo: Buffalo Historical Society, 1910), 220–221.

56. Hundreds of unsorted canal packet boat passenger lists, including the one cited here, may be found in the New York State Archives, Comptroller's Office—Other Canal Records, "Lists of passengers on boats on the Erie Canal, 1827–1829," A1057, Box 4.

57. Alan Taylor, *The Civil War of 1812: American Citizens, British Subjects, Irish Rebels, & Indian Allies* (New York: Alfred A. Knopf, 2010), 443 (hereafter cited as Taylor, *Civil War of 1812*).

58. Taylor, *Civil War of 1812*, 253–258.

59. Jon Latimer, *1812 War with America* (Cambridge: The Belknap Press of Harvard University Press, 2007), 3.

60. Roger Jones, "Memoranda of a Military Tour Commenced at Brownsville on Sunday the 30th of May 1819, to Several Posts and Garrisons on the Waters of the Western Lakes," in *Publications of the Buffalo Historical Society*, vol. 24 (Buffalo: Buffalo Historical Society, 1920), 301–302. Note: Jones's journal was published by the Buffalo Historical Society in 1920 with the permission of the Library of Congress, where the original resided and still resides today.

61. Sedgwick's journal entry is quoted in Thomas A. Chambers, *Memories of War: Visiting Battlegrounds and Bonefields in the Early American Republic* (Ithaca: Cornell University Press, 2012), 131 (hereafter cited as Chambers, *Memories of War*).

62. James J. Talman, "A Secret Military Document, 1825," *The American Historical Review* 38.2 (January 1933): 294–300. My thanks to Paul R. Huey, Historical Archeologist, for bringing this article to my attention.

63. Chambers, *Memories of War*, 128.

64. Laura Auricchio, *The Marquis: Lafayette Reconsidered* (New York: Vintage Books, 2014), 296–297.

65. Journal entry dated Monday, September 11.

66. Journal entry dated Friday, September 29.

67. Raymond J. O'Brien, *American Sublime: Landscape and Scenery of the Lower Hudson Valley* (New York: Columbia University Press, 1981), 124 (hereafter cited as O'Brien, *American Sublime*).

68. O'Brien, *American Sublime*, 124.

69. O'Brien, *American Sublime*, 124–125.

70. O'Brien, *American Sublime*, 125.

71. Steven E. Kagle, *Early Nineteenth-Century American Diary Literature* (Boston: Twayne, 1986), 1–2 (hereafter cited as Kagle, *American Diary Literature*).

72. Kagle, *American Diary Literature*, 2–3.

73. Kagle, *American Diary Literature*, 2.

74. Kagle, *American Diary Literature*, 4.

75. Kagle, *American Diary Literature*, 5.

76. Ronald J. Zboray and Mary Saracino Zboray, "Books, Reading, and the World of Goods in Antebellum New England," *American Quarterly* 48.4 (December 1996): 588.

77. Tony Horwitz, *Blue Latitudes: Boldly Going Where Captain Cook Has Gone Before* (New York: Henry Holt and Company, 2002), 25.

78. Thanks to Vicki Weiss, Senior Librarian, Manuscript and Special Collections, who provided the journal's acquisition information. The seller was Howgate's Book Shop (no longer in business) of Schenectady, New York. Alexander Stewart Scott's original journal is cataloged under his name and call number BD13145.

79. Matthew DeLaMater, "Expedition New York," *New York Archives* 15.1 (Summer 2015): 11–15.

80. For the evolution and use of capitalization, see David Crystal, *The Cambridge Encyclopedia of the English Language*, 2nd ed. (Cambridge, UK: Cambridge University Press, 2004), 67.

The 1826 New York State Travel Journal of Alexander Stewart Scott

Preface

1. "As past participle: called (so-and-so), named, styled," s.v. "yclept | ycleped, adj." "Called," s.v. "yclep."

2. It is very difficult to read Scott's handwriting here. What can be deciphered appears to read "Jean [John] Bte [Baptiste?] Malars habal-baz." Given the sense of humor Scott exhibits in some of his journal entries, it seems probable that his "signature" is intended to be tongue-in-cheek.

Chapter One

1. The steamboat *Chambly* was one of the vessels owned and operated by the Saint Lawrence Steamboat Company. Scott is one of nineteen cabin passengers listed on the ship's manifest for August 2, 1826. Additionally, there were some 124 steerage passengers—presumably the "settlers" to whom he refers. See TheShipslist website at: http://www.theshipslist.com/ships/passengerlists/1826/caug02.shtml, accessed April 24, 2018. The phrase "upper Country" refers to Upper Canada, that portion of the country west of Montreal, bordering Lakes Ontario, Erie, Huron, and Superior. In 1791, the British government "divided the Province of Quebec into Lower Canada (on the lower reaches of the St. Lawrence River) and Upper Canada, along the present-day Ontario-Québec boundary." This division lasted until 1841 when the two were united, forming the Province of Canada. See Roger Hall, revised by Richard Foot, "Upper Canada," last edited March 4, 2015, in *The Canadian Encyclopedia Historica Canada*, 1985– , http://www.thecanadianencyclopedia.ca/en/article/upper-canada/, accessed April 24, 2018.

2. Three Rivers is the English name for the settlement founded in 1634 on the north shore of the Saint Lawrence River. It is located halfway between Quebec and Montreal where the Rivière Saint-Maurice flows into the Saint Lawrence. A three-pronged delta formed here by the river gave the community its name, which in French is "Trois Rivières." Refer to René Hardy, Claire-Andrée Fortin, and Norman Seguin, "Trois-Rivières," last edited March 4, 2015, in *The Canadian Encyclopedia Historica Canada*, 1985– , http://www.thecanadianencyclopedia.ca/en/article/trois-rivieres/, accessed April 24, 2018.

3. James Guthrie Scott (1803–1840) was Scott's older brother. In 1826, James is listed as an advocate (or lawyer) in Montreal. See *The Quebec Almanack and British American Royal Kalendar, for the Year 1826, Being the Second After Leap Year* (Quebec: Neilson & Cowan, 1825?), 69, HathiTrust Digital Library at: https://babel. hathitrust.org/cgi/pt?id=aeu.ark:/13960/t4km00316;view=1up;seq=74 (original from University of Alberta), PDF (hereafter cited as *Quebec Almanack, 1826*). "Harry" was Henry Stewart Scott (1807–1883), one of Scott's younger brothers. Just three months prior to Scott's arrival in Montreal, Edmund Bailey O'Callaghan, an Irish immigrant who had studied medicine for two years in Paris, France, was officially appointed to the position of Apothecary and Steward at the Montreal General Hospital. The large, three-story hospital, located on the outskirts of Montreal, formally opened in May 1822 with a capacity of seventy-two patients. O'Callaghan's demanding duties at the hospital required him to live in a small house on the hospital grounds. See Jack Verney, *O'Callaghan: The Making and Unmaking of a REBEL*, Carleton Library Series no. 179 (Ottawa: Carleton University Press, 1994), 24 (hereafter cited as Verney, *O'Callaghan*). O'Callaghan was officially licensed to practice medicine in November 1827. Soon afterward, he moved to Quebec, where he established his own practice, staying there until 1833, when he returned to Montreal to assume the editorship of the newspaper *Irish Vindicator*. See Maureen Slattery Durley, "Dr. Edmund Bailey O'Callaghan, His Early Years in Medicine, Montreal, 1823–1828," Canadian Catholic Historical Association, *Study Sessions*, 47 (1980), available online at www.cchahistory.ca/journal/CCHA1980/Durley.pdf, 29–39, accessed April 24, 2018. How Scott became acquainted with him is unknown, but their friendship clearly endured: not only is he frequently mentioned in the journal, but he was a witness at Scott's December 1830 marriage, in Quebec City, to Catherine Susan Fremont.

4. This was the Notre-Dame Basilica, construction of which began in 1824. Designed by American architect James O'Donnell in the Gothic Revival style, the church, completed in 1829, remains an architectural landmark of Montreal. See Alan Gowans, "Notre-Dame de Montreal," *Journal of the Society of Architectural Historians* 11.1 (March 1952): 20–26.

5. In 1826, an Edward Burroughs is listed as an advocate (or lawyer) in the Province of Quebec and a Charles Frémont is listed as a judge in the Court of the King's Bench in Montreal. See *Quebec Almanack, 1826*, 61–62, 67–68,

6. Edmund Kean (1789–1833) was a famous English actor touring in Canada and the United States in 1826. Known for his melodramatic roles, Kean was charismatic, but "he sank as often as he soared." See Peter Tomson, "Acting and Actors from Garrick to Kean," in *The Cambridge Companion to British Theatre, 1730–1830*, ed. Jane Moody and Daniel O'Quinn (Cambridge, UK: Cambridge University Press, 2007), 12. *The Iron Chest* was written by English dramatist George Colman the Younger in 1796. Damian Walford Davies, writing about *The Iron Chest*, quotes from J. F. Bagster-Collins's 1946 book *George Colman the Younger, 1762–1836*: "Most of the greatest tragedians of the nineteenth century played it and scored personal triumphs. It . . . was one of Edmund Kean's greatest performances." See Damian Walford Davies, "The Politics of Allusion: 'Caleb Williams,' 'The Iron Chest,' 'Middlemarch,' and the Armoire de fer," *The Review of English Studies* 53.212 (November 2002): 532.

7. The "McCords" probably refers to the families of brothers William King McCord (1803–1858) and John Samuel McCord (1801–1865), both prominent in Montreal as lawyers and judges. It is very possible that Scott knew William King McCord, who was a law student in Quebec at the same time Scott was. Refer to: Jean-Claude Robert, "McCORD, WILLIAM KING," in *Dictionary of Canadian Biography*, vol. 8, University of Toronto/Université Laval, 2003–, http://www.biographi.ca/en/bio/mccord_william_king_8E.html, and "McCord Family Fonds (P001), Administrative History—Biographical Sketch," McCord Museum website at: http://collections.musee-mccord.qc.ca/scripts/explore.php?Lang=1&tableid=18&tablename=fond&elementid=17__true, both accessed July 12, 2016.

8. King's Bench. The Court of the King's Bench was established in 1794 as the sole superior court for the then colony of Canada. Refer to Jim Phillips, "A Brief History of the Court of the King's Bench for Upper Canada, 1791–1841," *Online Encyclopedia of Canadian Legal History of the Osgoode Society for Canadian Legal History*, at: http://www.osgoodesociety.ca/encyclopedia/a-brief-history-of-the-court-of-kings-bench-for-upper-canada-1791-1841/, accessed July 13, 2016.

9. "Inquiry, investigation, or examination," s.v. "enquête." *The New Cassell's French Dictionary* (New York: Funk & Wagnalls, 1971). Scott and his brother were likely attending inquiry hearings at the Court of the King's Bench.

10. A comedy, *A New Way to Pay Old Debts*, was written in 1633 by English playwright Philip Massinger (1583–1640). See Paul Harvey and Dorothy Eagle, eds., *The Oxford Companion to English Literature*, 4th ed. revised (New York: Oxford University Press, 1969), s.v. "Massinger, Philip."

11. "A gay, dashing fellow; a dandy, fop, 'fast' man," s.v. "bucks."

12. "The highest grade, degree, or quality," s.v. "first water." *Merriam-Webster's Collegiate Dictionary*, 11th ed. (Springfield: Merriam-Webster, 2003).

13. It is possible that the steam-powered "ferry boat" on which he crossed the St. Lawrence River was the *Montreal*, built in 1819–1820 "to run as a ferry

between Montreal and La Prairie, . . . the starting point for the stages to St. John's and the United States." See Frank Mackey, *Steamboat Connections: Montreal to Upper Canada, 1816–1843* (Montreal: McGill-Queen's University Press, 2000), 8.

14. Reverend Baldwyn was William D. Baldwyn, who served as the rector of St. James Church in St. John's, Quebec. See entry for "Egerton, Lebbeus," in *American Ancestry: Giving the Name and Descent, in the Male Line of Americans Whose Ancestors Settled in the United States Previous to the Declaration of Independence, A.D. 1776*, vol. 12 (Albany: Joel Munsell's Sons, 1899), 188, HathiTrust Digital Library at: https://babel.hathitrust.org/cgi/pt?id=hvd.32044098876048;view=1up;seq=192 (original from Harvard University), PDF (hereafter cited as *American Ancestry*).

15. Situated on the Richelieu River, the community of St. John's, Quebec, where Scott's parents lived at the time, is now called Saint-Jean-sur-Richelieu. An 1825 description notes, "Though a place of considerable business, it possesses nothing in its appearance or accommodations inviting to a stranger." See Gideon M. Davidson, *The Fashionable Tour, in 1825. An Excursion to the Springs, Niagara, Quebec and Boston* (Saratoga Springs: G. M. Davison, 1825), 140, HathiTrust Digital Library at: https://babel.hathitrust.org/cgi/pt?id=hvd.32044019971019;view=1up;seq=136 (original from Harvard University), PDF (hereafter cited as Davidson, *The Fashionable Tour*).

16. Scott's mother's name was Janet Erskine Scott (1771–1840). At the time of his visit, Scott's youngest sister, Elizabeth (Betsy), was staying in St. John's with their parents.

17. The Reverend Baldwyn's daughter's name was Jane. See *American Ancestry*, 188.

18. Scott's father was George Scott (1774–1837), who, in 1826, was employed as the "gauger," an officer of His Majesty's Customs at St. John's responsible for surveying goods liable for excise taxes. See *Quebec Almanack, 1826*, 87.

19. The garrison referred to by Scott was located at Fort Saint-Jean, situated on the Richelieu River. It was one of a series of strategically placed forts constructed and manned by the British army to deter possible American invasion from the south along what had once been referred to by Native Americans as "The Great Warpath." In their periodic struggles, throughout the eighteenth and early nineteenth centuries, to gain territorial control and dominance, French forces, Native American war parties, and British and American troops traversed and waged fierce battles all along the two-hundred-mile natural corridor shaped by the Hudson River, Lakes George and Champlain, and the Richelieu and St. Lawrence Rivers between Albany, New York, and Montreal, Quebec. At the time of Scott's journey, the War of 1812 had been over for eleven years, but British and Canadian forces still actively maintained defensive positions in case of further hostilities with the United States. For use of the term "the Great Warpath" and a history of conflict along it, see Eliot A. Cohen, *Conquered into Liberty: Two Centuries of Battles Along the Great Warpath That Made the American Way of War* (New York: Free Press, 2011), 2 (hereafter cited as Cohen,

Conquered into Liberty). For information about the fort, now a museum, see the Musée du Fort Saint-Jean Museum website at: http://www.museedufortsaintjean.ca/EN/histoire/britannique/britannique.htm, accessed July 13, 2016.

20. The Lake Champlain Steamboat Company began regularly scheduled trips between St. John's, Canada, and Whitehall, New York, in 1814, and constructed the 108-foot *Congress* in 1818. See Bellico, *Sails and Steam in the Mountains*, 264 and 267.

21. Here Scott spells Baldwin with an *i* instead of a *y*.

22. "In or with the family; as one of the family; at home," s.v. "en famille."

23. Lake Champlain steamboats left St. John's each Monday and Friday at 8 a.m. See Dwight, *Northern Traveller, 1825*, 129.

24. Eleven miles from St. John's and nine miles from Rouses Point in New York, the small island of Île-aux-Noix (Scott misspells the name), in the middle of the Richelieu River, was another tactical defensive site guarding against invasion from the United States. See Dwight, *Northern Traveller, 1825*, 138, and Parks Canada website, "Fort Lennox National Historic Site at: http://www.pc.gc.ca/eng/lhn-nhs/qc/lennox/index.aspx, accessed July 16, 2016.

25. The American fortification Scott mentions was begun in 1817 to guard against British invasion from Canada. However, "A new land survey under the Treaty of Ghent [which had ended the War of 1812] disclosed that the fort's location was partially on Canadian soil." This quotation is from Bellico, *Sails and Steam in the Mountains*, 228.

26. This may be Split Rock, identified in 1825 as "a curiosity" located about fifteen miles from Burlington and "part of a rocky promontory projecting into the lake, on the west side, about 150 feet, and elevated above the level of the water about 12 feet." See Davidson, *The Fashionable Tour*, 145.

27. The tavern where Scott and his fellow passengers put up in Shoreham, Vermont, was probably Larrabee's. From there a ferry ran to Ticonderoga, where "a conveyance" was provided to take passengers the three miles to the steamboat landing on Lake George. See Davidson, *The Fashionable Tour*, 100 and 96.

28. The Lake George Steamboat Company built the 125-ton *Mountaineer* in 1824. Reputedly painted red, white, and blue, it operated on the lake for thirteen seasons. See Bellico, *Sails and Steam in the Mountains*, 300.

29. Scott's attribution of the origin of the name of Sabbath Day Point, while popularly believed, is inaccurate. The name was applied to the spot much earlier than the Revolutionary War and its origins are unknown. For the Lord Amherst origin, see Theodore Dwight, *The Northern Traveller: Containing the Routes to Niagara, Quebec, and The Springs, with the Tour of New-England, and the Route to the Coal Mines of Pennsylvania* (New York: A. T. Goodrich, 1826), 171, HathiTrust Digital Library at: https://babel.hathitrust.org/cgi/pt?id=loc.ark:/13960/t9377t28z;view=1up;seq=225 (original from Library of Congress), PDF (hereafter cited as Dwight, *Northern Traveller, 1826*). For the earlier use and unknown origin of the name, see Seneca

Ray Stoddard, *Lake George; A Book of To-day*, 12th ed. (Albany: Van Benthuysen & Sons, 1882), 113, HathiTrust Digital Library at: https://babel.hathitrust.org/cgi/pt?id=hvd.hx4tc9;view=1up;seq=139 (original from Harvard University), PDF; and also Russell P. Bellico, *Chronicles of Lake George: Journeys in War and Peace* (Fleischmanns, NY: Purple Mountain Press, 1995), 63 (hereafter cited as Bellico, *Chronicles of Lake George*).

30. "Flavor or savour of food," s.v. "gout."

31. The source of Scott's quotation has not been identified.

32. "A bugle fitted with keys to increase the range of sounds it can produce," s.v. "key bugle."

33. Caldwell Village is today the village of Lake George, New York. See Ren Vasiliev, *From Abbotts to Zurich: New York State Placenames* (Syracuse: Syracuse University Press, 2004), 126.

34. James Fenimore Cooper's novel *The Last of the Mohicans* was published on February 4, 1826, just six months prior to Scott's journey. The novel's great popularity is evidenced by Scott's familiarity with it and the tourist attraction that "Cooper's Cave" in Glens Falls, New York, had already become. The United States Hotel in 1826 is described as "a fine building of brick, three stories high, with a colonnade rising only to the second story. This house is excellently well kept, and is more substantially built than any of the rest . . ." See Dwight, *Northern Traveller, 1826*, 149.

35. Toward the front of his bound journal, Scott kept a page that he headed "Memoranda." Here he entered the names of individuals he encountered during his journey. The transcription of this page may be found in appendix 1. Mr. Phoenix heads the list of names, possibly because he was the first Scott wanted to remember, and is listed as "Mr. D. A. Phoenix, 71 Front St. N. York." Longworth's 1826 city directory for New York City lists Daniel A. Phoenix as residing at that address. He seems to have been a merchant. See *Longworth's American Almanac, New-York Register, and City Directory for the Fifty-First Year of American Independence* [. . .] (New York: Thomas Longworth, 1826), 380, HathiTrust Digital Library at: https://babel.hathitrust.org/cgi/pt?id=osu.32435056191703;view=1up;seq=408;size=75 (original from The Ohio State University), PDF (hereafter cited as *Longworth's American Almanac*).

Chapter Two

1. The college to which Scott refers is Union College, founded in 1794. See Horatio Gates Spafford, *A Gazetteer of the State of New-York:*[. . .]. Facsimile of the 1824 edition, with preface by Warren Broderick (Interlaken, NY: Heart of the Lake Publishing, 1981), 474 (hereafter cited as Spafford, *Gazetteer*).

2. Scott wrote down Dr. Moore's name and address, "48 Warren St. N. York," on a page at the front of his journal that he titled "Memoranda." Samuel W. Moore, M.D., is listed as residing at this address in Longworth's 1826 city directory for New York City. See *Longworth's American Almanac*, 344. The transcription of Scott's Memoranda entries, in which he jotted down the names and addresses of some of the people met during his journey, will be found in appendix 1.

3. In an 1826 advertisement for his hotel placed in the Utica newspaper *Oneida Observer*, A. Shepard "respectfully" announced to "his friends and customers, that he returns them many thanks for their liberal patronage the year past . . . where by his assiduous efforts to please, he hopes to merit and receive a share in the future." He offered "board by the day, week or month." In his 1892 history of Utica, Moses Bagg gives the innkeeper's full name as Abraham Shepard. Shepard's hotel name was variously spelled by contemporary travelers. Scott adds two *p*'s. Bernhard, Duke of Saxe-Weimer-Eisenach, who stayed there in August 1825, recorded its name as "Shepherd's" and wrote of Utica and its hotels: "It has also several ale-houses, and three fine taverns, at the largest of which, called Shepherd's hotel, we found excellent accommodations. In this house there are always more than seventy beds for the accommodations of strangers; and these on some occasions are barely sufficient." See "Utica Hotel," *Oneida Observer* (Utica, NY), April 18, 1826. Also see Moses Mears Bagg, *Memorial History of Utica, N. Y., From Its Settlement to the Present Time* (Syracuse: D. Mason & Co., 1892), 163 and 168, HathiTrust Digital Library at: https://babel.hathitrust.org/cgi/pt?id=coo1.ark:/13960/t61555f9m;view=1up;seq=193 (original from Cornell University), PDF (hereafter cited as Bagg, *Memorial History*). Also see Bernhard, Duke of Saxe-Weimer Eisenach, *Travels Through North America, During the Years 1825 and 1826*, vol. 1 (Philadelphia: Carey, Lea & Carey, 1828), 65, HathiTrust Digital Library at: https://babel.hathitrust.org/cgi/pt?id=nyp.33433 081776175;view=1up;seq=71 (original from the New York Public Library), PDF (hereafter cited as Bernhard, *Travels*).

4. "Coolness, indifference, absence of excitement or agitation," s.v. "Sang froid."

5. The Marquis de Lafayette, a French nobleman, who volunteered his services to the American army during the Revolutionary War. During that conflict, he rose to the rank of major general, served with great distinction, and became a popular American hero. He returned to the United States in August 1824 and undertook a triumphal tour through the country that lasted into September 1825. He arrived in Utica on June 10, 1825, and, according to Bagg's *Memorial History*, "breakfasted and dined at Shepard's." However, Auguste Levasseur, General Lafayette's secretary, who accompanied him on this trip, states in his 1829 published journal, "We only spent four hours at Utica; . . ." See John Davidson Godham, trans. Auguste Levasseur, *Lafayette in America in 1824 and 1825; or Journal of a Voyage to the United States*, vol. 2 (Philadelphia: Carey and Lea, 1829), 195, HathiTrust Digital Library

at: https://babel.hathitrust.org/cgi/pt?id=hvd.32044009577586;view=1up;seq=195 (original from Harvard University), PDF. See also Bagg, *Memorial History*, 168.

6. New York's Supreme Court of Judicature (its proper name from 1691 to 1847) held four terms a year. Prior to 1820, two of these terms were held in New York City and two in Albany; however, in that year, one of the court's terms was moved to Utica, where it convened during the month of August. Scott's arrival just at the time the court was in session was fortuitous. See *"Duely & Constantly Kept": A History of the New York Supreme Court, 1691–1847, and an Inventory of Its Records (Albany, Utica, and Geneva Offices), 1797–1847* (Albany: New York State Court of Appeals and the New York State Archives and Records Administration, 1991), 1, 4, 112.

7. The Emmet mentioned by Scott is Thomas Addis Emmet (1764–1827), an exiled Irishman who immigrated to New York in 1803 following the execution of his brother Robert, who had led a failed Irish rebellion against the British. Emmet was admitted to the New York State bar in 1805 and soon became an eminent lawyer. See the Historical Society of the New York Courts website entry for "Thomas Addis Emmet" at: http://www.nycourts.gov/history/legal-history-new-york/legal-history-eras-02/history-era-02-addis-emmet.html, accessed August 10, 2016.

8. Founded in 1816, the Auburn prison was the second such facility constructed by the state, the first being in New York City. In his 1869 history of Auburn, Henry Hall describes the facility as being "surrounded by a wall three thousand feet long, four feet thick, and varying . . . from twelve to thirty-five feet in height." He further elaborates that its buildings were "arranged in the form of a hollow square. . . . They consist of a central building, with wings which, being L-shaped, run back at right angles to the rear, and unite with rows of shops . . . . The main building is fifty-six feet high; the wings are forty-five . . ." The prison was, and remains today, an imposing part of Auburn. Henry Hall, *The History of Auburn* (Auburn, NY: Dennis Bro's & Co., 1869), 361–362.

9. Walter Grieve (1773–1826), a native of Dumfriesshire, Scotland, immigrated to the United States around 1794 and settled in Geneva. There, with a partner, John Moffatt, he established (circa 1803) Geneva's first brewery. Grieve also served as the village's first postmaster and fought in the War of 1812 as a lieutenant colonel and commandant of the Seventh Regiment, Third Brigade, of the New York State Artillery. In 1819 he was promoted to the rank of brigadier general of the Fourth Brigade of the New York State Artillery. For his military rank, refer to Hugh Hastings, ed., *Military Minutes of the Council of Appointment of the State of New York, 1783–1821* (Albany: James B. Lyon, 1901), vol. 2, 1387, and vol. 3, 2088. Also see Grieve's obituary and special notice of his death placed by the "New-York State Artillery, 4th Brigade," in *the Geneva Gazette and General Advertiser* (Geneva, NY), December 27, 1826. For Grieve's brewery and general background see, "Who Was Walter Grieve?," Genesee Country Village and Museum blog, http://gcvmblog.blogspot.com/2012/04/who-is-walter-grieve.html accessed May 4, 2018.

10. "A person, especially a man, who behaves in a dishonorable or contempt-ible way; someone worthless or despicable; a villain," s.v. "blackguard." Apparently at a later date, someone—perhaps Scott himself—penciled out his parenthetical phrase, "very much like English Blackguards."

11. This may have been John Scott Hogarth (1793–1861), who was a tailor in the village. See E. Thayles Emmons, *The Story of Geneva* (Geneva: The Finger Lakes Times, 1982), 417.

12. "Colloquial phrase, as bold as brass: very bold(ly) or impudent(ly); brazen-faced(ly)," s.v. "brass."

Chapter Three

1. As noted in the introduction, Scott's sister, Margaret Jane, and her hus-band, William Cunningham Batchelor, moved from Quebec to Palmyra, New York, sometime after 1821. William, who had previously acted as a merchant, and Scott during his visit made several side trips from Palmyra on "business," which suggests that he was pursuing some type of entrepreneurial opportunity in this rapidly grow-ing part of the state. In his travel journal, Scott never identifies the nature of his brother-in-law's business in Palmyra, nor has any information been found relating to Batchelor's activities in that community. In his 1824 *Gazetteer*, Horatio Gates Spafford writes that Palmyra "has long been a place of very considerable business, and is the third rank in this County [Wayne], and increasing rapidly." See Spaf-ford, *Gazetteer*, 400. Scott does not name which of his two older sisters (the second oldest, Ann Semple Austin Scott, was staying with the Batchelor family) did not immediately recognize him; however, in the intervening years since last seeing him, Scott had matured into young adulthood. For more information on Scott's family, refer to the introduction.

2. John W. Hallet was appointed judge of the Wayne County Court on April 19, 1825. Scott misspelled his last name. See George W. Cowles and H. P. Smith, *Landmarks of Wayne County New York* (Syracuse: D. Mason & Company, 1895), 107.

3. The June 18 issue of the Palmyra newspaper, *the Wayne Sentinel*, announced to its readers: "Theatrical!—Messrs. Gilbert and Trowbridge have arrived with their Company, and as will be seen by their advertisement [which ran on the same page], intend performing a few evenings in this village." According to their advertisement, their plays were mounted in "St. John's Assembly Room" with tickets priced at 25 cents. The assembly room was in the St. John's Hotel and Stage House. See *Wayne Sentinel* (Palmyra, NY), June 18, 1826. Clearly, Scott was unimpressed with their acting skills. The play titled "Mountaineers" was written and produced by English playwright George Colman the Younger in 1795. See Leslie Stephen, ed., *Dictionary of National Biography*, vol. 11 (London: Smith, Elder, & Co., 1887), s.v. "Colman, George, the younger," 394, HathiTrust Digital Library at: https://babel.hathitrust.

org/cgi/pt?id=nyp.33433082196407;view=1up;seq=407 (original from the New York Public Library), PDF. The other play Scott saw, "Bombastes Furioso," was "a long popular burlesque" first produced in 1810 by another English playwright, William Barnes Rhodes. See Sidney Lee, ed., *Dictionary of National Biography*, vol. 48 (London: Smith, Elder, & Co., 1896), s.v. "Rhodes, William Barnes," 85, HathiTrust Digital Library at: https://babel.hathitrust.org/cgi/pt?id=nyp.33433082197074;view=1up;seq=97 (original from the New York Public Library), PDF.

4. "The legal profession. Esp. in gentleman (also man, member) of the long robe: a lawyer, a barrister," s.v. "long robe."

5. "Brisk talk, conversation," s.v. "crack."

6. "To drink; esp. to drink slowly or in small portions, to sip," s.v. "tiff."

7. "Low Spirits." Eric Partridge, *A Dictionary of Slang and Unconventional English*, 5th ed. (New York: Macmillan Company, 1961), s.v. "blue devils."

8. The Batchelor children were: James Cunningham Batchelor, aged eight; George Scott Batchelor, aged four; Erskine Scott Batchelor, aged one year, four months; and Stewart Scott Batchelor, aged six months.

9. Scott is referring to the poem "The Scotch Elder's Sunday Ride," by Scottish poet Robert Burns (1759–1796).

10. The full title of the play Scott attended was *The London Merchant, or The History of George Barnwell*, a tragedy written and originally produced in 1731 by playwright George Lillo. See Sidney Lee, ed., *Dictionary of National Biography*, vol. 33 (London: Smith, Elder, & Co., 1896), s.v. "Lillo, George," 252, HathiTrust Digital Library at: https://babel.hathitrust.org/cgi/pt?id=nyp.33433082198312;view=1up;seq=266 (original from the New York Public Library), PDF.

11. "Church," s.v. "kirk."

12. Scott is most probably referring to the Reverend Benjamin B. Stockton, the minister of this church at the time of Scott's visit. See James Harvey Hotchkin, *A History of the Purchase and Settlement of Western New York; and of the Rise, Progress and Present State of the Presbyterian Church in That Section* (New York: M. W. Dodd, Brick Church Chapel, 1848), chap. 25, online at Wayne County GenWeb, "Early History of the Presbyterian Church to 1848 in Wayne County, Ontario County, Seneca County, and Yates County, NY," at: http://wayne.nygenweb.net/, accessed September 1, 2016.

13. King George IV, the reigning monarch of Great Britain, whose far-flung colonies included Canada.

14. "Drunk," s.v. "stewed."

15. Scott provides no clue about the nature of the business that took him to Geneva.

16. "Jail," s.v. "gaol."

17. "Immediately," s.v. "instanter."

18. "A fast or furious driver," s.v. "Jehu." Scott does not identify who Bob is; however, it might have been his fifteen-year-old brother, Robert F. Scott. In his journal entry for September 22, Scott writes of his travel to Sodus Bay, New York,

"to see about the situation for my Br. Bob." These are the only mentions of Bob in the travel journal.

19. Scott placed his nephew's name in parentheses.

20. The Reverend John A. Clark (without the *e* as Scott spells it) served Palmyra's Zion Episcopal Church from 1824 to 1826. See George W. Cowles and H. P. Smith, *Landmarks of Wayne County New York* (Syracuse: D. Mason & Company, 1895), 194.

21. "Early in the morning," s.v. "betimes."

22. The electors for the Town of Palmyra (in which the village of Palmyra was located), were meeting to select three delegates "to meet at Brown's Coffee House, in the Village of Newark, on Wednesday the 6th day of September next, . . ." See "Wayne County Convention," *Lyons Advertiser* (Lyons, NY), September 6, 1826.

23. "A small quantity or measure of alcoholic liquor, usually a quarter of a pint; a small drink of spirits," s.v. "noggin."

24. See Scott's entry for August 24, which notes that the Episcopalians were meeting in the local school house, hence the presence of desks.

25. On August 2, 1826, Daniel Webster delivered a eulogy at Boston's Faneuil Hall for John Adams and Thomas Jefferson, both of whom had died on July 4, 1826. Five days after Webster spoke, the Boston Common Council ordered seven thousand copies of Webster's speech to be printed "for the use of the citizens." Through the month of August 1826, New York newspapers widely reported the news of Adams's and Jefferson's deaths and on local commemoration ceremonies. They also printed excerpts of Webster's eulogy, noting that his entire speech had "been published, and forms a pamphlet of 62 pages." See "Webster's Eulogy," *Commercial Advertiser* (New York, NY), August 26, 1826. See also Daniel Webster, *A Discourse in Commemoration of the Lives and Services of John Adams and Thomas Jefferson, Delivered in Faneuil Hall, Boston, August 2, 1826* (Boston: Cummings, Hilliard and Company, 1826). Webster's speech is available in PDF format from the HathiTrust Digital Library at: https://catalog.hathitrust.org/api/volumes/oclc/654321.html.

26. The insertion of "Mem." in his entry here is intended to serve as a reminder to himself.

27. New York's militia were required by law to "rendezvous by companies in their respective beats, on the first Monday of September in every year, at nine o'clock in the forenoon, for the purpose of training, disciplining and improving in martial exercise; . . ." See "An Act to Organize the Militia, Passed April 23d, 1823, with Rules and Regulations, Forms and Precedents, Prescribed by the Commander in Chief, for the Use and Government of the Militia of the State of New-York" (Albany: Leake and Croswell, 1823), 12, HathiTrust Digital Library at: https://babel.hathitrust.org/cgi/pt?id=hvd.hx4rpl;view=1up;seq=50 (original from Harvard University), PDF.

28. Located about twelve miles to the southeast from Palmyra, the village of Vienna was characterized by Horatio Gates Spafford in his 1824 *Gazetteer* as "flourishing" and having "valuable mills." The village changed its name to Phelps in

1855. See Spafford, *Gazetteer*, 411; and Ren Vasiliev, *From Abbotts to Zurich: New York State Placenames* (Syracuse: Syracuse University Press, 2004), 176.

29. Captain Hotchkiss may have been Leman Hotchkiss, who in 1819 was quartermaster of the Twenty-fourth Brigade of Infantry of Ontario County. The obituary of a Major Leman Hotchkiss of Vienna, who died on December 31, 1826, appeared in the *Geneva Gazette* (Geneva, NY), Wednesday, January 3, 1827. See also Hugh Hastings and Henry Harmon Noble, eds., *Military Minutes of the Council of Appointment of the State of New York, 1783–1821*, vol. 3 (Albany: James B. Lyon, 1901), 2015.

30. "A drop in our eye" is slang meaning "To be slightly tipsy." See Eric Partridge, *A Dictionary of Slang and Unconventional English*, 5th ed. (New York: Macmillan Company, 1961), 243.

31. In his *Gazetteer* entry for Manchester Village, Horatio Gates Spafford writes that it "has some manufactures, a small collection of houses, the Post-Office, 'and an elegant stone Church, with a bell.'" He also observed that the village was located "on the post-road from Canandaigua to Palmyra." Scott and Batchelor were undoubtedly traveling on this post road. See Spafford, *Gazetteer*, 303. A post road was a route "designated by Congress for the carriage of mails." See Kimberly McCray, "postal service," in *The Encyclopedia of New York State*, ed. Peter Eisenstadt and Laura-Eve Moss (Syracuse: Syracuse University Press, 2005), 1230.

32. Spafford, writing about the Sulphur Springs in his 1824 *Gazetteer*, notes that the "Sulphurous Fountains. . . . have very justly attracted considerable notice . . . they emit great quantities of sulphuretted hydrogen, which diffuses the scent to very considerable distances." See Spafford, *Gazetteer*, 303. Spafford further records that the springs also were known by the name of Clifton Springs, the name of the community today. See also Ren Vasiliev, *From Abbotts to Zurich: New York State Placenames* (Syracuse: Syracuse University Press, 2004), 47.

33. "A bowling game . . . having nine pins in a diamond shaped configuration with one pin in the center," s.v. "ninepin." *Merriam-Webster's Collegiate Dictionary*, 11th ed. (Springfield: Merriam-Webster, 2003). Spafford in his description of the springs noted that the Clifton Hotel had good accommodations for visitors, and it is possible that it was at this hotel where Scott played his game of nine pins. See Spafford, *Gazetteer*, 303.

34. "The time when pudding or puddings are to be had; a time when a person is in luck; a favorable or useful time," s.v. "pudding time."

Chapter Four

1. The Eagle Hotel "situated in the main street" was described by Edward Thomas Coke, who visited Rochester in 1832, as "a fine hotel with excellent rooms and an attentive landlord." A portion of Coke's travel account (Edward Thomas

Coke, *A Subaltern's Furlough* [London: 1833], 279–283), including this quotation, is reprinted in Blake McKelvey, ed., "Part I—Foreign Travelers' Notes on Rochester and the Genesee Country before 1840," *The Rochester Historical Society Publications*, vol. 18 (Rochester: Rochester Historical Society, 1940), 53. Apparently, the Eagle Hotel also was recognized as a popular stop by other travelers. McKelvey includes two other mentions of it in accounts dating from 1828 and 1837 (pages 53 and 90).

2. The Erie Canal crossed the Genesee River at Rochester on what Horatio Gates Spafford in his 1824 *Gazetteer* called "a stupendous work, one of the most interesting features of the . . . Erie Canal." See Spafford, *Gazetteer*, 191.

3. Apparently, mills for the sawing of stone, especially marble, were not uncommon in the early nineteenth century. See Harley J. McKee, *Introduction to Early American Masonry, Stone, Brick, Mortar and Plaster* (Washington, DC: The National Trust for Historic Preservation, 1973), 30–31. Spafford undoubtedly refers to the stone formations at Rochester when he writes: "Extensive quarries of free stone have lately been discovered, near the Falls of Genesee, with which the Contractors are building the Aqueduct for the Erie Canal. The stone is much used in building." See Spafford, *Gazetteer*, 327.

4. Considerable attention is given to the Ridge Road by Spafford. He states that the road was also known as the Alluvial Way, a reference to the belief that this natural ridge, extending along the shore of Lake Ontario between the Genesee and Niagara Rivers, had been formed by the ancient receding of Lake Ontario waters. Spafford further notes that this ridge, being naturally even and quite smooth, made an ideal road and that "it was made a post road in 1817, and has a line of Post Coaches that carry the mail and passengers on it, between Lewiston and Canandaigua, by Rochester, 3 times a week." See Spafford, *Gazetteer*, 24.

5. "Honey and oatmeal mixed with whiskey (and water), sometimes with cream added," s.v. "Athole brose." Iseabail Macleod, Ruth Martin, and Pauline Cairns, eds., *Pocket Scots Dictionary* (Edinburgh: Polygon, an imprint of Edinburgh University Press, 1999).

6. Scott wanted to cross the Niagara River to Queenston, Canada (also spelled Queenstown in the early nineteenth century), directly opposite Lewiston, so he could travel the Canadian road running down the west side of the river to Niagara Falls. This route would enable him to visit the monument then being erected to commemorate the death of British Major General Sir Isaac Brock in the War of 1812. Brock had been killed repelling an American invasion from Lewiston, New York, during the Battle of Queenston Heights. Scott was mistaken when he wrote that Brock and two of his *aides-de-camp* (military officers assisting a superior officer), also killed in the battle, were buried in the monument. Only one aide, Lieutenant Colonel John Macdonell, was interred with Brock. See "History of Brock's Monument," The Friends of Fort George, http://www.friendsoffortgeorge.ca/brocks-monument/history/index.html, accessed September 7, 2016; "Major General Sir Isaac Brock, The Hero of Upper Canada (1769–1812)," Niagara Falls Museums, History

Notes, https://niagarafallsmuseums.ca/discover-our-history/history-notes/brock.aspx; and C. P. Stacey, "Brock, Sir Isaac," in *Dictionary of Canadian Biography*, vol. 5, University of Toronto / Université Laval, 2003, http://www.biographi.ca/en/bio/brock_isaac_5E.html, accessed September 7, 2016.

7. Scott had mistakenly jotted down "PM" here. From his journal entry, it is clear that it was 11 a.m. when Scott and his fellow travelers arrived, not 11 p.m.

8. The Eagle Tavern, located on the American side of the Niagara River in the village of Niagara Falls, New York, was operated by Parkhurst Whitney. In his 1834 guide to the area, Joseph Ingraham wrote of Whitney, "He is attentive to his guests, and knows how to accommodate and provide for them." See Joseph Wentworth Ingraham, *A Manual for the Use of Visitors to the Falls of Niagara:* [. . .] (Buffalo: Charles Faxon, 1834), 19, Google Books at: https://books.google.com/books?id=S4ErAAAAYAAJ&pg=PA39&dq=A+Manual+for+the+Use+of+Visitors+to+the+Falls+of+Niagara&hl=en&sa=X&ved=0ahUKEwiVxbji7orbAhVQzVMKHX54D2EQ6AEISzAH#v=onepage&q=A%20Manual%20for%20the%20Use%20of%20Visitors%20to%20the%20Falls%20of%20Niagara&f=false (original from Harvard College Library), PDF (hereafter cited as Ingraham, *Falls of Niagara*). See also Pierre Berton, *Niagara: A History of the Falls* (New York: Penguin Books, 1998), 37 (hereafter cited as Berton, *Niagara*).

9. Actually, Scott misidentified the island on which the paper mill he saw was located; it was Bath Island, not Goat Island. In 1834 the mill was described as "a substantial building 119 feet by 46, and 3 stories in height." Ingraham, *Falls of Niagara,* 56.

10. Scott's memory of these last three lines of stanza 25 from George Gordon Byron's (Lord Byron) poem "Childe Harold's Pilgrimage," canto 2, is not quite correct. The original lines published in 1812 are:

Alone o'er steeps and foaming falls to lean;
This is not solitude; 'tis but to hold
Converse with Nature's charms, and view her stores unroll'd.

See Jerome J. McGann, ed., *Lord Byron, The Complete Poetical Works*, vol. 2, *Childe Harold's Pilgrimage* (Oxford: Oxford University Press, 1980), 52 (hereafter cited as McGann, *Lord Byron*).

11. Scott is paraphrasing the English proverb "Too much of one thing is good for nothing." See William George Smith and Paul Harvey, *The Oxford Dictionary of English Proverbs*, 2nd ed. (Oxford: Oxford University Press, 1963), 665.

12. Scott has misspelled the name of the Pavilion Hotel, erected in 1822 by William Forsyth. This hotel, occupying land offering the best views of the falls, was already widely known for its luxury. Forsyth had just enlarged his establishment in 1826 by adding wings to the main, three-storied, wood-framed structure.

Forsyth's holdings also included "Table Rock, the famed outcrop near the edge of the Horseshoe Falls which offered the finest prospect of it." See Robert L. Fraser, "Forsyth, William (1771–1841)," in *Dictionary of Canadian Biography*, vol. 7, University of Toronto / Université Laval, 2003, http://www.biographi.ca/en/bio/forsyth_william_1771_1841_7E.html, accessed September 7, 2016.

13. Lord Byron's poem "Childe Harold's Pilgrimage," canto 2, published in 1812, from which Scott slightly misquotes. The first three lines of stanza 50 actually read:

> We gaze and turn away, and know not where,
> Dazzled and drunk with beauty, till the heart
> Reels with its fulness; . . .

See McGann, *Lord Byron*, 140.

14. A "vast chunk" of Table Rock had fallen into the river in 1818. Pierre Berton in his history of the falls writes that "this intimidating ledge of dolostone still projected fifty feet over the Falls—so close to the crest that one traveler felt he could almost dip his toe into the raging water (this distance was less than five feet). The bolder visitors crept to the very lip of the overhang . . ." Berton, *Niagara*, 33.

15. Mr. Brant has not been identified. Scott has placed his name in parentheses, but whether he added it to his entry later is impossible to determine. It is written in the same hand and the same ink.

16. Thomas Clark, also spelled Clarke with an *e* as Scott does, was a fellow Scottish immigrant to Canada. At the time of Scott's visit, Clark and his family lived in a large mansion on his estate overlooking Niagara Falls on the Canadian side. Although he fought on the British side during the War of 1812, while General Grieve fought on the American side, it was probably their common Scottish connections and business interests that made them sufficiently acquainted for Grieve to write a letter of introduction for Scott to Clark. In addition to his various business ventures, Clark also served on several provincial commissions tasked with studying improvements to navigation along the St. Lawrence River. He also served as a justice of the peace—hence his absence when Scott visited. See Bruce A. Parker and Bruce G. Wilson, "Clark, William," in *Dictionary of Canadian Biography*, vol. 6, University of Toronto / Université Laval, 2003, http://www.biographi.ca/en/bio.php?id_nbr=2806, accessed September 8, 2016.

17. Forsyth, as part of his hotel operations, enabled his more daring visitors to climb down (by a spiral staircase he maintained at Table Rock) and venture under the falls. Berton, *Niagara*, 33.

18. Once more quoting from Byron's "Childe Harold's Pilgrimage," canto 4, the last three lines of stanza 71 and the first line of stanza 72, Scott is a bit inaccurate. These lines read:

Lo! where it comes like an eternity,
As if to sweep down all things in its track,
Charming the eye with dread,—a matchless cataract,
Horribly beautiful! . . .

See McGann, *Lord Byron*, 148.

19. At this point in his journal, Scott drew a symbol to indicate the insertion point of the following lines of poetry by William Wordsworth that Scott wrote on a separate slip of paper and then pinned to the page:

> A step,
> A single step, which freed me from the skirts
> of the blind vapour, opened to view,
> Glory beyond all glory ever seen
> By waking sense, or by the dreaming soul!
> (Wordsworth)

English poet William Wordsworth's lines, which Scott quotes here, are from book 2, "The Solitary," lines 829–833, of the long poem "The Excursion," published in 1814. See E. De Selincourt and Helen Darbishire, eds., *The Poetical Works of William Wordsworth*, vol. 5 (Oxford: Oxford University Press, 1949), 71–72. Once more, Scott's rendering of the lines is slightly off. The actual lines are:

> . . . a step,
> A single step, that freed me from the skirts
> Of the blind vapour, opened to my view
> Glory beyond all glory ever seen
> By waking sense or by the dreaming soul!

20. Two meanings for the word "unco" could apply to Scott's usage here: "Unknown, strange; unusual" and "Remarkable, notable, great, large," s.v. "unco."

21. Halifax currency at this period of Canadian history was the standard in use there; however, grasping what it means precisely is a bit complicated. Briefly stated, "Halifax currency" did not comprise any form of coin or paper money; rather it was a rating system uniformly adopted in 1821 for the purpose of keeping accounts. Scott followed this practice and, as will be seen in appendix 2, he kept his travel-expense accounts in Halifax currency. As Robert Chalmers observes in his book *A History of Currency in the British Colonies*, "It is . . . carefully to be borne in mind that by 'Halifax currency' is meant merely that the denominations were (imaginary) pounds, shillings, and pence, with a 5 s. [shilling] rating for the dollar." See Robert Chalmers, *A History of Currency in the British Colonies* (London: Her Majesty's Stationery Office, 1893), 183, HathiTrust Digital Library at: https://

babel.hathitrust.org/cgi/pt?id=aeu.ark:/13960/t3cz3m01r;view=1up;seq=200 (original from University of Alberta), PDF.

22. From the context of his entry, it seems Scott uses the word "coo" to mean that he took a rest. "To send to rest, etc. by cooing," s.v. "coo."

23. "The part of the head on which the hair grows," s.v. "poll."

24. Mordecai Manuel Noah, the principal figure behind the 1825 effort to create a Jewish settlement on Grand Island, located in the Niagara River, has been characterized as the "foremost American-Jewish leader during the first half of the nineteenth century, . . . and the most prominent Jewish exemplar of Zionism in his day in the United States." He was far from the derogatory characterization of being "cracked in the upper story" repeated by Scott. The settlement, dedicated with the name Ararat, was envisioned as a city of refuge for Jews from all over the world for "the revival and reestablishment of the 'government of the Jewish Nation, under the auspices and protection of the constitution of the United States of America,' with Noah as 'Governor and Judge of Israel.'" His proclaimed role in the settlement was not well received, nor was there international Jewish support of immigration to the proposed new settlement. Noah's visionary project ended in failure. See Louis Ruchames, "Mordecai Manuel Noah and Early American Zionism," *American Jewish Quarterly* 64.3 (March 1975): 195, 212–218.

Chapter Five

1. In his 1824 gazetteer of the state, Spafford noted that the Niagara River was "about ¾ of a mile wide, and runs with a very strong current." He also stated that the cost of the ferry from the Canadian side to Black Rock, was "25 cents for a single person, . . ." See Spafford, *Gazetteer*, 52–53.

2. The Eagle Tavern is the only one of the four "large" inns specifically mentioned by name in Theodore Dwight's 1826 edition of *The Northern Traveller*. See Dwight, *Northern Traveller, 1826*, 99.

3. In one of the more infamous events of the War of 1812 between the United States and Great Britain, American forces, who since June 1813 had occupied the British Fort George located across the Niagara River in Canada, retreated in the face of advancing British troops on December 10–11 of the same year. During their retreat, they burned the adjacent Canadian community of Niagara (also known as Newark and today called Niagara-on-the-Lake) to the ground, leaving some four hundred residents homeless in the middle of winter. In rapid and furious retaliation, the British launched a surprise night attack on Fort Niagara, taking it silently with their bayonets. Quickly following up that victory, on December 30, they launched a two-pronged attack on Black Rock and Buffalo, New York, destroying the latter community. See Robert Malcomson, *Historical Dictionary of the War of 1812* (Lanham, MD: Scarecrow Press, 2006), s.v. "Buffalo, New York," 66, and

s.v. "Niagara, UC, The Burning of (10–11 December 1813)," 374–376. See also Richard V. Barbuto, *Niagara 1814: America Invades Canada* (Lawrence: University Press of Kansas, 2000), 1–2, 90–92.

4. The canal packet boat *Utica*, which Scott took passage on, was undoubtedly operated by the Erie Canal Packet Boat Company, which advertised a Buffalo departure at 8 a.m. daily during the 1826 season. See "Erie Canal Packet Boats," advertisement in *the People's Press* (Batavia, NY), September 23, 1826.

5. This is a word where Scott's original handwriting causes some confusion, for he has clearly written "François," which translates into English as the proper name Francis. From the context of his sentence, this makes no sense. However, the same word spelled with an *a* instead of an *o* (Français) translates to English as "Frenchman," which fits Scott's meaning: the father was a complete Frenchman. See *The New Cassell's French Dictionary* (New York: Funk & Wagnalls, 1962), s.vv. "François" and "Français."

6. Strategically located in Canada at the entrance to the Niagara River from Lake Erie, Fort Erie was a British fortification that changed hands several times during the War of 1812. See Robert Malcomson, *Historical Dictionary of the War of 1812* (Lanham, MD: Scarecrow Press, 2006), s.v. "Erie, Fort," 169. Of the two lighthouses that Scott records seeing, one was among the first to be built by the federal government on the Great Lakes. It was constructed at Buffalo in 1818. See Eric Jay Dolin, *Brilliant Beacons: A History of the American Lighthouse* (New York: Liveright, 2016), 85. The second light has not been identified.

7. As Spafford records in his 1824 *Gazetteer*, the Erie Canal ran from Buffalo Creek along the Niagara River to Tonawanda Creek, ten miles from Buffalo, where "the Creek forms the Canal these 12 miles, . . . at the end of this distance a deep cut commences, which extends 7½ miles, in a NEasterly direction, across what is called the *Mountain Ridge*, with about 3 miles of rock, averaging 20 feet in depth, . . ." See Spafford, *Gazetteer*, 169.

8. In their 1825 report to the legislature, the New York State Canal Commissioners enthused about the nearly completed combined locks at Lockport: "This is a work of the first magnitude on the line, and one of the greatest of the kind in the world." Both Theodore Dwight's *The Northern Traveller* and Henry Dilworth Gilpin's *A Northern Tour*, published in 1825, included the Canal Commissioners' text verbatim. See *Laws of the State of New York, in Relation to the Erie and Champlain Canals,*[. . .], vol. 2 (Albany: E. and E. Hosford, 1825), 245, HathiTrust Digital Library at: https://babel.hathitrust.org/cgi/pt?id=njp.32101065133090;view=1up ;seq=253 (original from Princeton University), PDF (hereafter cited as, *Laws of New York, 1825*); Dwight, *Northern Traveller, 1825*, 155–156; and Henry Dilworth Gilpin, *A Northern Tour: Being a Guide to Saratoga, Lake George, Niagara, Canada, Boston, &c.*[. . .] (Philadelphia: H. C. Carey & I. Lea, 1825), 142, HathiTrust Digital Library at: https://babel.hathitrust.org/cgi/pt?id=umn.31951001683695b;vi

ew=1up;seq=154 (original from University of Minnesota), PDF (hereafter cited as Gilpin, *A Northern Tour*).

9. Where precisely Scott came by these figures is unknown. Actual construction of the deep cut and the double combination five locks at Lockport extended from May of 1821 through October of 1825, when water finally was let through the entire area. Regarding the number of workmen employed in the construction, historian Patrick McGreevy persuasively states that "the few workforce estimates we have always rounded off to the nearest five hundred (e.g., one thousand or fifteen hundred) only shows what crude guesses they were." He suggests that actual numbers might have exceeded two thousand, although adding, "the paucity of evidence makes it impossible to draw a firm conclusion." See Patrick McGreevy, *Stairway to Empire: Lockport, the Erie Canal, and the Shaping of America* (Albany: State University of New York Press, 2009), 41–104. McGreevy, provides definitive detail on the construction at Lockport; page 95 is the source of the quotations on the estimated number of workers.

10. Dwight, in the second edition of his popular guidebook, *The Northern Traveller*, published in 1826, notes under his entry for Lockport that "collections of minerals may be purchased here." See Dwight, *Northern Traveller, 1826*, 79. The excavation of the Erie Canal across the state revealed a heretofore unrivaled cross section of the state's mineral resources along with its geological and fossil history, in which the work of pioneering natural scientists like Amos Eaton served to heighten public interest. For an excellent study on this topic, see David I. Spanagel, *DeWitt Clinton and Amos Eaton: Geology and Power in Early New York* (Baltimore: Johns Hopkins University Press, 2014).

11. In his original entry, Scott inserted an asterisk at this point and at the bottom of the page added the following: "as might be expected I never again heard of them—S.S." The initials, S.S., are Scott's. While his proper full name was Alexander Stewart Scott, he apparently often used his middle name, hence these initials stand for Stewart Scott.

12. The Oak Orchard Falls and the canal aqueduct crossing Oak Orchard Creek were located just north of Medina, New York. The aqueduct is described briefly in the Canal Commissioners' report of 1825: "Across the Oak Orchard creek an aqueduct of sixty feet span has been constructed of stone, in a most substantial manner, . . ." See *Laws of New York, 1825*, 244, and Arad Thomas, *Pioneer History of Orleans County, New York* (Albion: H. A. Bruner, 1871), 372, HathiTrust Digital Library at: https://babel.hathitrust.org/cgi/pt?id=yale.39002029511293;view=1up; seq=400 (original from Yale University), PDF.

13. Scott does not describe how this accident happened; perhaps it occurred so quickly that he didn't witness the events leading up to it. However, he does say it happened because of "some mismanagement on the part of both drivers," meaning the men or boys on the tow path driving the teams of Scott's packet boat and

the canal boat that was passing "coming up." Since "up" boats were heading west and "down" boats were heading east to market, this tells us that the boats involved were passing in opposite directions. Packet boats, like the one Scott was on, had the right of way. The canal tow path ran on only one side of the canal, meaning that traffic moving in both directions shared it. Very probably what happened is that the driver of the west-bound boat failed to stop his team in time to allow that boat's tow line to drop into the water, partially submerging it so that the packet boat could safely pass over it. Instead the still taut line came across the deck of the packet boat and caught the reading passenger sitting on deck, hurling him into the air, then smashing him to the deck. The following 1852 passage clearly describes how passing was supposed to work:

> As the two sets of horses approached, the line-boat horses turned off the path a little, on the side of the path farthest from the canal, and then stopped a moment so as to allow the packet-horses to go by them. The horses were stopped a moment, in order to let the tow-rope, which they were pulling, fall down upon the path, so that the packet-horses could step over it easily. Then, when the boats approached each other [a team and its driver were anywhere from 100 to 110 feet ahead of the boats they were pulling], the helmsman on board the line-boat steered his boat out, away from the tow-path, and the helmsman of the packet steered his in, toward the tow-path. By this means the rope of the line-boat came exactly across in the way the packet was to go, and it seemed as if it was going to cut across the packet's bows. But just before the bows of the packet came against the rope, the boy who was driving the line-boat horses, stopped a moment, and as the line-boat kept moving on after the horses had stopped, it caused the tow-rope to drop down in the water, and it sunk so low that the packet-boat sailed directly over it, without difficulty.

See Jacob Abbott, *Marco Paul's Voyages & Travels: Erie Canal* (New York: Harper & Brothers, 1852), 65–66.

14. The rate of toll for packet boats in 1825 was set at six cents per mile. See *Laws of New York, 1825*, 259.

15. Presumably this is the same Edward Burroughs who Scott mentions in his journal entry of August 5.

16. The nephews, to whom Scott refers here, were George Scott Batchelor and Erskine Scott Batchelor, aged four years and sixteen months, respectively.

17. "An acute or high fever; disease, or a disease, characterized by such fever, especially when recurring periodically, specifically malaria. Also: a malarial paroxysm, or (especially in later use) the initial stage of such a paroxysm, marked by an intense feeling of cold and shivering," s.v. "ague."

18. "Time flies," s.v. "tempus fugit."

19. It seems possible that prior to the wedding a celebratory dinner was held at the hotel. The local Palmyra newspaper, *the Wayne Sentinel*, carried a notice of their marriage in its Friday, September 22, 1826, issue. It read: "MARRIED—In this village on Saturday last, by F. Smith, Esq. [,] Gen. WALTER GRIEVE, of Geneva, to MISS ANN SCOTT, of this village." This was General Grieve's second marriage. His first wife, Janet (Jean) Walsh, died just a year earlier on September 19, 1825. See entry for Grieve burials in "Pulteney Street Cemetery, Geneva NY" at: http://freepages.genealogy.rootsweb.ancestry.com/~darmi/pulteneystcem.html, accessed September 18, 2016. Scott's sister Ann's marriage was very short lived; Grieve died less than three months later on December 21, 1826. *The Geneva Gazette, and General Advertiser* of Wednesday, December 27, 1826, published his obituary:

> DIED—In Geneva, on Thursday morning last, in the 53d year of his age, Walter Grieve, Esq., Brigadier General of the 4th Brigade, New York State Artillery. Gen. Grieve was a native of Dumfriesshire, Scotland; he emigrated [*sic*] to the United States and settled in this village about thirty-two years ago, having been one of its first settlers; at which period there were but three houses in the place. On Saturday his remains were interred with Military honors, being attended to the grave by detachments of Artillery and Light Infantry, and Officers of Artillery and other corps in uniform, and by a large concourse of citizens.

20. Fred S. Hall, looking at the history of common law marriages in New York State, writes: "In no state has the doctrine of common law marriage had so varied and significant a history as in New York. For more than half a century after the Revolution all marriages were common law marriages in the eyes of the law, for no marriage statutes were in existence." In his article, Hall provides the following quotation, citing, *Report of the Committee on the Judiciary of the Assembly* in 4 Legislative Documents of the Senate and Assembly of the State of New York (1830), Doc. No. 361 (Serial Vol. No. 114):

> Although marriage before the adoption of the late Revised Statutes was only a civil contract, capable of being effectually made in the presence of any competent witness, yet . . . it has been the habit of our citizens to summon the ministers of the gospel to bear witness to this sacred compact rather than to call to witness the civil functionaries of the land.

While General Grieve and Ann Scott did not follow this particular "habit," the quotation confirms the accuracy of Scott's remarks. See Fred S. Hall, "Common Law Marriage in New York State," *Columbia Law Review* 30.1 (January 1930): 1, 4.

21. "John Henry Hobart (September 14, 1775–September 12, 1830) was appointed Bishop of the New York State Episcopal Diocese in 1816. In his efforts

to reinvigorate the church, he made many visits across the state. It was certainly during one of these visits that Scott heard him. See Robert Bruce Mullin, "Hobart, John Henry," in *The Encyclopedia of New York State*, ed. Peter Eisenstadt and Laura-Eve Moss (Syracuse: Syracuse University Press, 2005), 723–724.

Chapter Six

1. Scott's phrase "to see about the situation for my Br." refers to a job possibility that he wishes to investigate for his fifteen-year-old younger brother Robert Scott (1811–1878). No further mention of this is made in the journal, so anything more about the potential position for Bob is unknown. The fact that Scott's brother-in-law, William Batchelor, accompanied him suggests that it may have been Batchelor, as a locally connected businessman, who either had heard of the job opening or arranged for Scott to meet Mr. Dolloway, the person apparently doing the hiring. The village of Sodus on the "Great Sodus bay, reckoned the best harbor on the S. shore of Lake Ontario; . . . ," was located about twelve miles north of Lyons, according to Spafford. See Spafford, *Gazetteer*, 493.

2. A William Dolloway is listed as an early settler of Sodus Bay, where in 1826 he was a founding member of the Episcopal church there, contributing the substantial amount of $200 toward the construction of its building. As Scott's sister and her husband, William Batchelor, were active in the Episcopal church in Palmyra, this may explain how Batchelor and Scott knew of a possible job opening with Dolloway. Unfortunately, Dolloway was not at home when Scott and Batchelor arrived in Sodus Bay. See George W. Cowles, ed., *Landmarks of Wayne County, New York* (Syracuse: D. Mason & Company, 1895), 206, 218–219. For Dolloway's contribution to the local Episcopal church, see Lewis H. Clark, *History of the Churches of Sodus* (Sodus: 1876), 56.

3. The Sodus Bay Lighthouse was about a year old when Scott saw it, having been completed in 1825. See Scott C. Monje, "Sodus Point," in *The Encyclopedia of New York State*, ed. Peter Eisenstadt and Laura-Eve Moss (Syracuse: Syracuse University Press, 2005), 1435.

4. "Disposed to anger or easily angered; hot-tempered, fiery; bad-tempered, irascible; irritable, cantankerous. Also: characterized by or indicative of such a temperament," s.v. "choleric."

5. "In a state or fit of indignation or offence; with indignation or offence," s.v. "dudgeon."

6. Scott is quoting almost verbatim from Spafford's *Gazetteer*, 461. The informative canal boat captain could have lent a copy of the book to Scott, or perhaps Scott was carrying it with him.

7. Spafford, *Gazetteer*, 375.

8. Elisha Wallace of Syracuse, New York, is one of the names Scott entered in the page he entitled "Memorandum." The transcription of Scott's Memorandum

page can be found in appendix 1. Wallace, who was thirty-five years old when Scott met him, had come to Syracuse in 1825 to practice law but became a "large salt manufacturer." See Dwight H. Bruce, *Onondaga's Centennial*, vol. 1 (Boston: The Boston History Company, 1896), 437.

9. ". . . but long live the English girls!" My thanks to independent scholar Margaret Lynch-Brennan for helping translate this French phrase. Looking at a copy of the original entry—Scott's handwriting is particularly difficult to decipher in this particular entry—Lynch-Brennan states: "I think what he is saying is 'mais vivent les Anglaises' which idiomatically, but not literally, means 'but long live the English girls.'" Margaret Lynch-Brennan email message to the editor, June 28, 2016.

10. Scott has inserted this cross-reference to page 20 in his journal for his first extensive description of Little Falls in his entry dated August 17.

11. "Called." s.v. "yclep." "As past participle: called (so-and-so), named, styled," s.v. "yclept | ycleped, adj."

12. Scott does not give a first name for Mr. De Graff. Since many members of the De Graff family lived in Schenectady, it is difficult to know to which De Graff his letter of introduction is addressed. However, it was most likely John Isaac DeGraff (1783–1848), especially since he was a practicing lawyer and major political figure in the city and Scott was always eager to talk with other lawyers. Further, the letter of introduction was from Scott's new brother-in-law, General Grieve, a War of 1812 veteran likely to be familiar with John Isaac DeGraff, who had played an important role in that conflict. For more information on John I. DeGraff, see Jim Strosberg, "Schenectady's First Elected Mayor," *Schenectady County Historical Society Newsletter* 56.11–12 (November–December 2013), accessible online at: http://schenectadyhistorical.org/admin/wp-content/uploads/2013/10/Nov-Dec-2013a.pdf, accessed June 27, 2016.

13. "Immediately, forthwith, at once. (Originally and still technically a law term, but now chiefly an emphatic substitute for *instantly*.)," s.v. "instanter."

14. Leverett Cruttenden's establishment, formally called Congress Hall but popularly known by his name, was located at the corner of Park Place and Washington Street near the Capitol. In their 1886 history of Albany County, Howell and Tenney assert that prior to its removal in 1878, Cruttenden's hotel was the "chief hotel of the city." They also state that his hotel "was the headquarters of the legal fraternity, members of the Legislature, and all distinguished travelers." See George Rogers Howell and Jonathan Tenney, eds., *Bi-Centennial History of Albany: History of the County of Albany, N. Y., from 1609 to 1886* [. . .] (New York: W. W. Munsell & Co., 1886), 651–652.

Chapter Seven

1. Theodore Dwight's 1826 guidebook, *The Northern Traveller*, states that the population of Albany in 1825 was 15,954. See Dwight, *Northern Traveller, 1826*, 43.

2. Both Dwight's *The Northern Traveller* and Spafford's *Gazetteer* give the length of the Albany basin as four thousand feet. Spafford, noting that it was not yet completed in 1824, records its width varying from eighty to three hundred feet. The quay or pier to which Scott refers was, according to Spafford, eighty feet wide; Dwight characterizes it as "wide enough for a spacious street." See Dwight, *Northern Traveller, 1826*, 49; and Spafford, *Gazetteer*, 15.

3. Scott may have inadvertently made an error in writing down the number of "sloops and schooners" navigating the Hudson River when he recorded "3 [,000]–4000." The actual number was undoubtedly much fewer. Spafford observed, "The shipping, including that annually paying wharfage in this City, amounts to about 400, principally sloops . . ." It seems likely that Scott simply added an extra zero to this estimate. Spafford, *Gazetteer*, 15–16. Spafford's figure is consistent with the following numbers given for Troy, New York, and published in *The American Annual Register; for the Years 1826–27*: "The trade of this thrifty and beautiful city, during the last season [1826], gave full employment to eighty sloops and schooners, measuring on an average, more than 75 tons each, besides tow-boats and other transport boats, performing the business of 30 sloops of 100 tons each, in addition." See *The American Annual Register; for the Years 1826–27* (New York: E. & G. W. Blunt, 1828), 461, HathiTrust Digital Library at: https://babel.hathitrust.org/cgi/pt?id=nyp.33433081899571;view=1up;seq=469 (original from New York Public Library), PDF.

4. The Albany Academy, constructed in 1815–1816, and still standing today, was a boys' school. It was designed by the well-known and highly regarded Albany architect Philip Hooker (1766–1836). See Douglas G. Bucher and W. Richard Wheeler; Mary Raddant Tomlan and Ruth Osgood Trovato, eds., *A Neat Plain Modern Stile: Philip Hooker and His Contemporaries, 1796–1836* (Clinton: Trustees of Hamilton College; Amherst: University of Massachusetts Press, 1993), 38 (hereafter cited as Bucher, *Philip Hooker*).

5. Also designed by Philip Hooker, the New York State Capitol (constructed 1806–1809 and altered 1818) provided space for both state and city government functions until 1831, when city offices moved out. See Bucher, *Philip Hooker*, 96–100. In his 1824 *Gazetteer* Spafford devotes considerable space to a description of the Capitol:

> This building stands at the head of State street, adjoining the public square, and on an elevation of 130 feet above the level of the Hudson. It is a substantial stone building, faced with free stone taken from the brown sand stone quarries on the Hudson below the Highlands. . . . On the right, at the west end of the hall, you enter the Assembly-Chamber, which is 56 feet long, 50' wide, and 28 in height. . . . It has a gallery supported by 8 antique fluted Ionic columns;—the frieze, cornice, and ceiling piece, (18 feet diameter,) are richly ornamented in Stucco. From

this hall, on the left, you are conducted to the Senate-Chamber, 50 feet long, 28 wide, and 28 feet high, finished in much the same style as the Assembly-Chamber. In the furniture of these rooms, with that of the Council of Revision, there is a liberal display of public munificence, and the American Eagle assumes an Imperial splendor.

From Spafford, *Gazetteer*, 13.

6. Spafford's description of the "attic story" of the Capitol notes that it: "contains a Mayor's Court Room, a room for the Society of Arts, for the State Library, and the State Board of Agriculture." See Spafford, *Gazetteer*, 13. The State Library, created by legislation in 1818, was "envisioned . . . not merely as an adjunct of government and the courts, but as a general reference library as well." In 1822, the library's collections included "1,406 volumes and 369 pamphlets . . ." See Cecil R. Roseberry, *For the Government and People of This State: A History of the New York State Library* (Albany: University of the State of New York, the State Education Department, 1977), 4, 7.

7. In his description of the Capitol, Spafford did not exclude the cupola from which Scott surveyed the surrounding countryside:

The building is roofed with a double-hip, or pyramidal form, upon the centre of which is erected a circular cupola, 20 feet diameter, covered with a domical roof, supported by 8 insulated columns, of the Ionic order, and contains a small bell for the use of the courts.

From Spafford, *Gazetteer*, 13.

8. Governor DeWitt Clinton resided in his own home located at the corner of North Pearl and Steuben Streets. See George Rogers Howell and Jonathan Tenney, eds., *Bi-Centennial History of Albany: History of the County of Albany, N. Y., from 1609 to 1886* [. . .] (New York: W. W. Munsell & Co., 1886), 443.

9. Scott's sense of local, popular opinion regarding Clinton's chances of becoming President of the United States in the 1828 election and of Andrew Jackson being a "mere soldier and not fit for the place" proved wrong. For a discussion of the political maneuvering around the 1828 election that saw Clinton's hopes dashed, those of rival New York politician Martin Van Buren realized, and the "mere soldier" elected president, see Daniel Walker Howe, *What Hath God Wrought: The Transformation of America, 1815–1848* (unnumbered vol.) in *The Oxford History of the United States*, ed. David M. Kennedy (New York: Oxford University Press, 2007), 240–241, 275–284.

10. The federal arsenal was (and is today) located north of Albany adjacent to the community of Gibbonsville (now Watervliet) on the same side of the Hudson River. Theodore Dwight's 1826 guide, *The Northern Traveller*, provides a wonderful description of the process of gaining entrance to the arsenal (although

he mislabels it as a state facility) and gives more details of what Scott undoubtedly saw during his visit:

> Strangers may easily gain access by mere application at the officers' quarters. These are in the south wing of the principal building, which faces the road and the river; and the remainder of which is occupied for the storing of arms. The lower floor is devoted to such arms as are intended for supplying the military posts, or have been received for repairing. The arms in the second loft are disposed with more taste. The muskets are partly packed in boxes, and partly ranged upright, with fixed bayonets, in compact order; and present an appearance truly formidable. Thousands of pistols are hung over head; those in the alternate lines standing different ways; and swords with metallic scabbards are disposed horizontally on wire hooks. The walls are ornamented by several devices formed of swords, pistols, &c. ingeniously arranged.

Clearly, Scott was less impressed than Dwight. See Dwight, *Northern Traveller, 1826*, 51.

11. Dwight in his lengthy description of the Watervliet Arsenal also identifies the cannon on which Scott comments:

> In the yard are a number of cannon, &c. There are 4 medium 12 pounders, one 24, and one howitzer, all taken at Saratoga [referring to the 1777 battle of Saratoga, New York, where the American army defeated the British]; 4 medium 12 pounders, and one howitzer taken at Yorktown [referring to the October 19, 1781, surrender of the British under the command of General Charles Cornwallis to a combined American and French force]; two long antique pieces and one 3 inch mortar taken at Stony Point [referring to the 1779 battle at Stony Point, New York, where a daring American night attack took a British stronghold]; two old French 4 pounders and 14 guns, sent by King Louis to the Continental Congress in the revolution. These are all of brass, and most of them highly ornamented.

See Dwight, *Northern Traveller, 1826*, 52.

12. While no reference contemporary to Scott's visit has been located for the Mechanic Hall, ten years later in a state gazetteer it was among those hotels listed in the city of Troy as being "most distinguished." See Thomas F. Gordon, *Gazetteer of the State of New York:* [. . .] (Philadelphia: T. H. and F. G. Collins, 1836), 650, HathiTrust Digital Library at: https://babel.hathitrust.org/cgi/pt?id=yale.39002005 201448;view=1up;seq=774 (original from Yale University), PDF.

13. "The two principal county courts were the court of common pleas (civil) and the court of general sessions of peace (criminal). The bench of these courts consisted of one first judge and several assistant judges (after 1818 the number was fixed at four). In most counties a quorum was one judge and two assistants." See *"Duely & Constantly Kept": A History of the New York Supreme Court, 1691–1847, and an Inventory of Its Records (Albany, Utica, and Geneva Offices), 1797–1847* (Albany: New York State Court of Appeals and the New York State Archives and Records Administration, 1991), 104.

14. The actual designation was "first judge." In Rensselaer County, the first judge in 1826 was David Buel Jr. See Franklin B. Hough, *The New York Civil List,* [. . .] (Albany: Weed, Parsons & Co., 1858), 363, HathiTrust Digital Library at: https://babel.hathitrust.org/cgi/pt?id=nnc2.ark:/13960/t2n60dj1x;view=1up;seq=389 (original from Columbia University), PDF.

15. "A man's great-coat or overcoat," s.v. "surtout."

16. This was probably Mount Ida. Theodore Dwight in his 1826 guide writes: "On Mount Ida, a hill east of Troy, is a fine succession of water falls, on a stream which has cut its way in some places to a great depth, and takes three or four perpendicular leaps at short intervals of only a few yards." Henry Dilworth Gilpin's 1825 guide adds: "About two miles to the east of Troy is a fine cascade, known by the name of Mount Ida falls. It is formed by the Posten-kill, a stream which rushes from the high lands, and pouring down through wild ravines and woody dells, affords a scene which will attract the admiration of the lovers of the picturesque." See Dwight, *Northern Traveller, 1826*, 52, and Gilpin, *A Northern Tour*, 56–57.

Chapter Eight

1. This was Geurt Van Schoonhoven (1765–1847), a prominent resident of Waterford and Saratoga County. He fought as an enlisted man in the Revolutionary War and, thereafter, rose steadily through the ranks of the state militia, serving as the commander of the 144th Regiment during the War of 1812 and being promoted to the rank of major general in 1819. When Scott met him, he was serving as a judge of the Saratoga County Court of Common Pleas. See Violet B. Dunn, Robert S. Hayden, and Clayton H. Brown, eds., *Saratoga County Heritage* (n.p.: Saratoga County, 1974), 506. See also *New York in the Revolution as Colony and State*, 2nd ed., vol. 1 (Albany: J. B. Lyon Company, 1904), 234, HathiTrust Digital Library at: https://babel.hathitrust.org/cgi/pt?id=cool.ark:/13960/t6pz5sf5z;view=1up;seq=278 (original from Cornell University), PDF. For Van Schoonhoven's military ranks after the Revolution, see Hugh Hastings and Henry Harmon Nobel, eds., *Military Minutes of the Council of Appointment of the State of New York, 1783–1821*, vols. 1–3 (Albany: James B. Lyon, 1901), vol. 1, 114, 254, 350, 609; vol. 2, 1469, 1657;

vol. 3, 1956, 2022, HathiTrust Digital Library at: https://catalog.hathitrust.org/Re cord/001262454?type%5B%5D=all&lookfor%5B%5D=Military%20Minutes%20 of%20the%20Council%20of%20Appointment%20of%20the%20State%20of%20 New%20York%2C%201783-1821&ft=ft (originals from New York Public Library), PDF. For Van Schoonhoven's court of common pleas position, see E. R. Mann, *The Bench and Bar of Saratoga County* [. . .] (Ballston: Waterbury and Inman, 1876), 377, HathiTrust Digital Library at: https://babel.hathitrust.org/cgi/pt?id=mdp.35 112101783837;view=1up;seq=383 (original from University of Michigan), PDF.

2. This was probably Ezra Williams, whose name and address Scott recorded in his "Memoranda" page. See appendix 1 for the transcription of his complete entry. Scott noted Williams's address as Russia Iron Works in Clinton County. In 1829 Ezra Williams was the postmaster of Russia Iron Works. While no documentary evidence has been found, it seems likely that he was also involved in the iron ore mining and forging industry then thriving in the Champlain Valley. See *A Register of the Officers and Agents, Civil, Military, and Naval, in the Service of the United States on the 30th of September, 1829* [. . .] (Washington, DC: William A. Davis, 1830), *93 (note: an asterisk precedes the page number in the original), HathiTrust Digital Library at: https://books.google.com/books?id=LOdIAQAAIAAJ&pg=PR1& dq=A+Register+of+the+Officers+and+Agents,+Civil,+Military,+and+Naval,+in+the+Se rvice+of+the+United+States+on+the+30th+of+September,+1829&hl=en&sa=X&ved= 0ahUKEwiEqK_op4rbAhUC7oMKHa8yC-cQ6AEIMTAC#v=onepage&q=Ezra%20 Williams&f=false (original from Stanford University), PDF (hereafter cited as *A Register of Officers*). For information on the iron industry and Ezra Williams's pos sible connection with it, see George F. Bixby, S. Norton, and Marie Parcello Bixby, "The History of the Iron Ore Industry on Lake Champlain," *Proceedings of the New York State Historical Association* 10 (1911): 171–237, especially 227.

3. Not only was the upper Hudson River and the Champlain Valley, through which Scott was passing, "classic ground," as he phrases it, but it had been histori cally contested ground, fought over by the Native Americans, French, British, and Americans. Horatio Gates Spafford in his 1824 pocket guide to New York canals wrote of this region:

> It should be observed, in passing, that the military works of that day, walls of earth, thrown up in haste, are found on nearly all the summits of the River hill, from a little below Bemus's [*sic*] heights to fort Miller, and some above, principally, however, thence northward, on the east side of the Hudson. Many of them may be seen from the Canal, and the Stage road, a very pleasant one, close along side.

See Horatio Gates Spafford, *A Pocket Guide for the Tourist and Traveller, Along the Line of the Canals and the Interior Commerce of the State of New York*, 2nd ed. (Troy: William S. Parker, 1825), 71–72, HathiTrust Digital Library at: https://

babel.hathitrust.org/cgi/pt?id=mdp.39015081795083;view=1up;seq=77 (original from University of Michigan), PDF (hereafter cited as Spafford, *A Pocket Guide, 1825*).

4. Fought on October 7, 1777, the Battle of Bemis Heights (a strongly fortified American position on high ground) was a "brilliant success" for American forces and was a key factor leading to British General John Burgoyne's surrender, a major American victory. See Eric H. Schnitzer, "The Tactics of the Battle of Saratoga," in *The Saratoga Campaign: Uncovering an Embattled Landscape*, ed. William A. Griswold and Donald W. Linebaugh (Lebanon, NH: University Press of New England, 2016), 62–68; 65 (hereafter cited as Griswold, *Saratoga Campaign*).

5. "The Field of Grounded Arms," where on October 17, 1777, the British army formally surrendered, is located "about a mile south of the village of Saratoga" (today's Schuylerville). See Scott Stull, Michael Rogers, and Len Tantillo, "The Surrender and Aftermath of the Battles," in Griswold, *Saratoga Campaign*, 167.

6. British General Simon Fraser was mortally wounded on October 7, 1777, and was buried in the British fortification known as the Great Redoubt, "which most historians define as being comprised of three fortifications built by British and German troops on bluffs overlooking the Hudson River . . ." See Dean R. Snow, "The British Fortifications," in Griswold, *Saratoga Campaign*, 96. In the early nineteenth century, Fraser's grave was apparently well marked (as it remains so today as part of the Saratoga National Historic Park). In his chapter, Snow references archaeologist Galen Ritchie's report that engineers working on the construction of the Champlain Canal in 1817 "had used the Fraser burial site as a datum point." He further writes: "To this evidence can also be added a sketch made by Benson Lossing from a canal boat in the 1840s. . . . It shows the burial site with a curving fence that tracks . . . the route of the 1777 funeral procession." Griswold, *Saratoga Campaign*, 97, and Snow's footnotes 34 and 35 on page 104.

7. The community of Sandy Hill changed its name to Hudson Falls in 1910. See R. Paul McCarty, "Hudson Falls," in *The Encyclopedia of New York State*, ed. Peter Eisenstadt and Laura-Eve Moss (Syracuse: Syracuse University Press, 2005), 737.

8. Hudson River.

9. Scott's description of the canal construction he observes is rather confusing as are the now archaic identifying names he uses. The North River refers to the Hudson River. The Grand Northern Canal refers to the Champlain Canal, completed in 1823 and running from its junction with the Erie Canal near Cohoes (Albany County), New York, to Whitehall (Washington County)—Scott's destination. The canal he saw under construction was initially intended to provide additional water to the Champlain Canal. Later improvements to this feeder canal enabled boat traffic to and from Glens Falls, and it became known as the Glens Falls Feeder Canal. Horatio Gates Spafford in his 1825 guide to the state's canals describes this location: "Proposed Navigable Feeder, 7 miles in length, from the Hudson R. above Glen's Falls, not yet finished." See Spafford, *A Pocket Guide, 1825*, 74.

10. This is the same vessel that Scott took from St. John's, Canada, at the start of his journey. See his journal entry for Saturday, August 12, 1826. Spafford provides the following information of the boat's schedule from Whitehall: "The *Lake Champlain Steam-Boat* leaves Whitehall, for St. John's, every Thursday and Saturday, at 2 P.M., touching at all the intermediate places; fare, through, 8 dollars; . . ." See Spafford, *A Pocket Guide, 1825*, 25.

11. Edward Livingston, whom General Van Schoonhoven introduced to Scott, never served as a judge of the Louisiana Supreme Court. Either Scott misunderstood, or Van Schoonhoven did and was not corrected by Livingston. However, Livingston (1764–1836) was a towering judicial intellectual with broad governmental experience both at the state and federal levels. Among his many accomplishments at the time when Scott spoke with him were his contributions in Louisiana toward codification of its Civil Code and Code of Practice, contributions that "greatly enhanced his reputation as a leader in the field of jurisprudence." See William B. Hatcher, *Edward Livingston: Jeffersonian Republican and Jackson Democrat*, Southern Biography Series, ed. Wendell Holmes Stephenson and Fred C. Cole (Baton Rouge: Louisiana State University Press, 1940), 284.

12. Located north of Whitehall, the descriptive "Fiddler's Elbow" refers to "a short and sudden curve in the channel of the lake where high rocks project into the water." See *Vermont, the Land of Green Mountains* (Essex Junction: Vermont Bureau of Publicity, 1913), 154, HathiTrust Digital Library at: https://babel.hathitrust.org/cgi/pt?id=nyp.33433081902672;view=1up;seq=162 (original from New York Public Library), PDF.

13. Here Scott refers to his earlier journal entry of Monday, August 14, 1826, when he was first traveling down Lake Champlain from St. John's, Canada, at the beginning of his trip.

14. Scott is referring to the Battle of Plattsburgh, primarily a naval engagement, fought between the British and Americans on September 11, 1814, which resulted in an American victory. The British flagship *Confidence* mounted thirty-seven cannons; the American flagship *Saratoga* mounted twenty-six. No vessel mounted thirty-two as Scott records, nor was any named the *Essex*. As Bellico states, after the battle, the American commander sent both the captured *Confidence* with other smaller British vessels and the *Saratoga* "to winter quarters in Whitehall." See Bellico, *Sails and Steam in the Mountains*, 210, 214; 227. A full description of the battle will be found on pages 218–227. In his 1824 *Gazetteer*, Spafford, in his entry for Whitehall, notes the abandoned vessels there: "The vessels taken from the British, during the late war, as well as those that gained the victory, now repose in the *mud* [italics in the original], near Whitehall Village, objects of inquiry and attention with every *patriotic* [italics in the original] tourist and traveler." See Spafford, *Gazetteer*, 569.

15. Dr. Anderson is another name that Scott entered in his Memoranda page (see appendix 1). There he recorded that Anderson was a medical doctor and a professor residing at Troy or Burlington, Vermont. This was very likely William Anderson who

is listed as the Professor of Anatomy and Physiology in the medical department of the University of Vermont in Burlington from 1825 to 1828. Prior to that, Anderson served on the medical faculty of Middlebury College in Middlebury, Vermont, where, according to its 1821 catalog, he was a "Member of Royal College of Surgeons of Edinburgh." See *General Catalogue of the University of Vermont and State Agricultural College, Burlington, Vermont, 1791–1900* (Burlington: Free Press Association, 1901), 22, HathiTrust Digital Library at: https://babel.hathitrust.org/cgi/pt?id=mdp.39015075 097439;view=1up;seq=22 (original from University of Michigan), PDF, and *Catalogue of the Officers and Students of Middlebury College, and Vermont Academy of Medicine* [. . .] (Poultney: Smith & Shute, 1823), n.p., Ancestry.com. *U.S., College Student Lists, 1763–1924*, accessed September 29, 2016, original from *College Student Lists*, digitized by the American Antiquarian Society, Worcester, Massachusetts.

16. "A branch of medical science that deals with the sources, nature, properties, and preparation of drugs." *Merriam-Webster's Collegiate Dictionary*, 11th ed., s.v. "materia medica."

17. Dr. Maguire has not been identified.

18. It is unclear what Scott means here by his reference to "the visitors," unless he is simply referring to those people occasionally visiting the city and who are not permanent residents.

19. "The beginning of a 'new era' or distinctive period in the history of mankind, a country, an individual, a science, etc.," s.v. "epocha."

20. The "works" to which Scott refers were Fort Lennox, under construction from 1819 to 1829 "to guard the Canadian frontier against the Americans, . . ." See Bellico, *Sails and Steam in the Mountains*, 229.

21. Saint-Jean-sur-Richelieu in the province of Quebec, Canada.

22. At this location in his journal, at the top of the page, Scott attached, with a straight pin, a separate slip of paper on which he wrote: "N.B. Here what may be called my Travels End, and what is contained in the remaining pages can hardly prove even in the smallest degree interesting—I ought in fact at this place to have closed my Journal, only just as a kind of amusement, and really never intending it to be seen by others than my Relations, resolved to keep it going until I reached Quebec—so I make no apology for the perhaps more than common dryness of what may follow to any one who may choose to continue their perusal. S.S." The initials "N.B." stand for nota bene, " 'Note well' (used to draw attention to something important in a written text)," s.v. "N.B." The initials "S.S." are Scott's and stand for Stewart Scott, as he often did not use his full name of Alexander Stewart Scott.

Chapter Nine

1. This could be William Hallowell of Montreal, who in 1829 was listed as a justice of the peace for the district of Montreal. This identification seems likely,

as Scott's brother, James, who also lived in Montreal, was in legal practice there. See *The Montreal Almanack, or Lower Canada Register, for 1829, Being First After Leap Year* (Montreal: H. H. Cunningham, 1828), 27, HathiTrust Digital Library at: https://babel.hathitrust.org/cgi/pt?id=aeu.ark:/13960/t6252g93t;view=1up;seq=63 (original from University of Alberta), PDF (hereafter cited as *Montreal Almanack*)

2. Gabriel Marchand settled in St. John's (also known as Dorchester in the early nineteenth century) in 1803, becoming one of the community's earliest merchants and "a pioneer of the timber trade in the Richelieu region." His business profited from the demand for timber for shipbuilding during the War of 1812, in which he served, and after 1816 he was able to retire "to the countryside near Dorchester, to a fine farm on the banks of the Richelieu . . ." See Lionel Fortin, "Marchand, Gabriel," in the *Dictionary of Canadian Biography*, vol. 8, University of Toronto / Université Laval, 2003– , http://www.biographi.ca/en/bio/marchand_gabriel_8E. html, accessed October 3, 2016.

3. Yamaska Mountain would be visible from St. John's. "Bellisle" could be the mountain (also visible from St. John's) "frequently called Chambly and Beloeil; but most correctly Mount Rouville. . . . On the summit of this mountain there is a beautiful little lake of fine clear water, . . ." See Joseph Bouchette, *A Topographical Description of the Province of Lower Canada* [. . .] (London: W. Faden, 1815), 208, 216, HathiTrust Digital Library at: https://babel.hathitrust.org/cgi/pt?id=aeu. ark:/13960/t0dv2cj8g;view=1up;seq=239 (original from University of Alberta), PDF.

4. The idea of a canal making the connection Scott mentions here was first raised in 1819, but construction proceeded by fits and starts until the Chambly Canal, as it was called, was finally completed in 1843. See William Kingsford, *The Canadian Canals: Their History and Cost, with an Inquiry into the Policy Necessary to Advance the Well-Being of the Province* (Toronto: Rollo & Adam, 1865), 18–20, HathiTrust Digital Library at: https://babel.hathitrust.org/cgi/pt?id=mdp.39015063 961125;view=1up;seq=28 (original from University of Michigan), PDF.

5. "Dear wife," s.v. "cara sposa."

6. The original Lake Champlain Steamboat Company's vessel named *Phoenix* burned in 1819. The steamboat to which Scott refers here was the 150-foot craft named *Phoenix II*, completed in 1820. See Bellico, *Sails and Steam in the Mountains*, 267.

7. "To send to rest, etc. by cooing," s.v. "coo." From the context of his entry, it seems that Scott uses the word "coo" to mean that he and his father took a rest.

8. This is a cross-reference to his journal entry dated August 15.

9. While Scott misspells the name, he is referring to the Scottish author Sir Walter Scott's internationally popular novel titled *Waverley*, published in 1814. See Paul Harvey and Dorothy Eagle, eds., *The Oxford Companion to English Literature*, 4th ed. (New York: Oxford University Press, 1969), s.v. "Waverley."

10. His comment on James Fenimore Cooper's "other productions" suggests that Scott had read one or more of the novels Cooper had written prior to the 1826 publication of *The Last of the Mohicans*.

11. Whist was a popular game of cards. Janet E. Mullin writes, "Cards, in particular, lent themselves to the leisure hours of the middle classes. The ever-widening variety of card games and the relative cheapness and easy portability of a pack of cards made them an ideal way to pass the time. Any number of people could and did amuse themselves at different games in all sorts of settings and occasions." See Janet E. Mullin, *A Sixpence at Whist: Gaming and the English Middle Classes, 1680–1830* (Rochester, NY: Boydell & Brewer, 2015), 32 (hereafter cited as Mullin, *A Sixpence at Whist*).

12. "Advanced in years," s.v. "stricken."

13. "One who gains, makes profits, or derives advantage," s.v. "gainer."

14. Benjamin Silliman, a pioneer in the field of natural history at Yale, visited St. John's in 1819 and again sometime before 1824. His impression of the community, where Scott's parents lived, and of the British fortifications there, expand Scott's descriptions: "St. John's is a place in which a stranger will not wish to remain long. Although the country is fertile about it, its appearance is mean, dirty and disagreeable. A few troops are stationed here, but the ancient fort, which was very extensive, and still looks very venerable, with its high earthen walls and falling barracks, is an interesting ruin." See Benjamin Silliman, *Remarks Made on a Short Tour Between Hartford and Quebec, in the Autumn of 1819*, 2nd ed. (New Haven: S. Converse, 1824), 400, HathiTrust Digital Library at: https://babel.hathitrust.org/cgi/pt?id=aeu.ark:/13960/t1gj09j6q;view=1up;seq=437 (original from University of Alberta), PDF.

15. Another thirteen years passed until the fortifications once again were repaired and strengthened. See "British Colonial Era, 1760–1775 and 1776–1839," Musée du Fort Saint-Jean website at: http://www.museedufortsaintjean.ca/EN/histoire/britannique/britannique.htm, accessed October 3, 2016.

16. Miss Heath has not been identified.

17. Mr. Woods has not been identified.

18. Dr. Morton has not been identified.

19. St. Albans is in Vermont.

20. Under the recipe for Mushroom Ketchup, published in 1840, is found the following: "If you love good ketchup, gentle reader, make it yourself, . . . and you will have a delicious relish for made-dishes, ragouts, soups, sauces, or hashes." The anonymous author continues, warning about the mushrooms being used: "Take care they are of the right sort, and fresh gathered." See *The Cook's Own Book, and Housekeeper's Register* [. . .] (Boston: Munroe and Francis, 1840), 117.

21. The name Epsom Salts originates from the English town of Epsom where the mineral magnesium sulfate occurs. It is a "powerful laxative and cathartic." See

Daniel A. Goldstein, *The Historical Apothecary Compendium*, s.v. "Epsom Salts," and "Magnesil sulpha(ti)s, (, sol.)(, sulut.)" (Atglen, PA: Schiffer, 2015).

22. Given the context in which Mr. Adams's name appears, it seems possible that this was J. H. Adams, Deputy Commissary General of the Commissary of Accounts Department of the British army. See *Quebec Almanack, 1826,* 208.

23. Situated in the middle of the Richelieu River, the Île-aux-Noix (Scott consistently misspells it as "Isle aux Noix" throughout his journal) was a strategic location in the navigation route along which the contending armies of France, Britain, and then the United States moved from the eighteenth through the early nineteenth centuries. A series of fortifications were constructed on the island beginning in 1759. After the War of 1812, the British built the present Fort Lennox over the years from 1819 to 1828; it was occupied by the British army until 1870. When Scott visited the fort, it was garrisoned by the Seventieth Regiment (Surrey Regiment of Foot). See "Fort Lennox, National Historic Site of Canada," Canada's Historic Places, the Canadian Register at: http://www.historicplaces.ca/en/rep-reg/place-lieu.aspx?id=12608&pid=0, accessed October 5, 2016; *Fort Lennox, Ile-aux-Noix, Quebec . . . ,* Historic Sites series no. 3 (Ottawa: Department of the Interior, 1936), 3–28; "Unit History: 70th Regiment of Foot," Forces War Records at: https://www.forces-war-records.co.uk/units/4686/70th-regiment-of-foot/, accessed October 5, 2016.

24. Mr. Wyatt has not been identified.

25. Early.

26. St. John's Fort on the Richelieu was a key British defensive fortification constructed to protect the natural invasion route from the rebellious American colonies just over the border. In 1775 American forces commanded by General Montgomery used that route to invade the province of Quebec hoping that French Canadians would join them in taking up arms against the British. However, the Americans "badly misjudged Canadian sentiment." The troops manning the fort withheld an American siege lasting forty-five days before being forced to surrender. Their stubborn resistance significantly slowed and weakened the American invasion forces, ultimately resulting in the collapse of the campaign and a full-scale American retreat. For a brief overview of this action, see D. N. Sprague, revised by Richard Foot, "American Revolution—Invasion of Canada," last edited March 4, 2015, in the *Canadian Encyclopedia Historica Canada,* 1985– , http://www.thecanadianencyclopedia.ca/en/article/american-revolution/, accessed April 26, 2017. For information on the fort, refer to "Fort Saint-Jean National Historic Site of Canada," Canada's Historic Places, the Canadian Register at http://www.historicplaces.ca/en/rep-reg/place-lieu.aspx?id=13294&pid=2635&h=Fort,SaintJean, accessed October 5, 2016, and "British Colonial Era 1760–1775 et 1776–1839," Musée du Fort Saint-Jean website at http://www.museedufortsaintjean.ca/EN/histoire/britannique/britannique.htm, accessed October 5, 2016. Scott later determines that these mounds were indeed graves.

27. The number that Scott has placed in parenthesis is a cross-reference to the page number of his journal entry dated Thursday, September 28, when he first meets Dr. Anderson.

28. The British actor Edmund Kean, whose performances Scott attends and records in his journal entries of Saturday, August 5, and Monday, August 7.

29. In 1831, Jay Langdon is listed as the Deputy Collector and Inspector of US Customs in Burlington, Vermont. See *A Register of Officers*, 33.

30. Mr. Hollwell, as the last name is spelled by Scott, has not been identified. However, it is possible that he has misspelled the last name, for there are both a J. M. Holwell and a W. Holwell listed as clerks in the Ordnance Department at Montreal. See *Montreal Almanack*, 119.

31. "A department for the supply of food and equipment," s.v. "commissariat." The dictionary definition adds the important point that "in the British Army, the Commissariat was a civilian service controlled by the Treasury until 1869."

32. As historian Janet Mullin explains, "Whist was a trick-playing game played by two sets of partners and a full deck of fifty-two cards. Whist was a relatively slow, strategic game involving several hands (rubbers), which allowed time for careful thought and discouraged impulsive play." See Mullin, *A Sixpence at Whist*, 180.

33. A "Chr. Collis" is listed as an assistant surgeon in the Seventy-Sixth (or Hindoostan) Regiment. See *Quebec Almanack, 1826*, 216.

34. It seems probable that his reference here to a "button hunt" refers to looking for mushrooms. A button mushroom is a young mushroom.

35. Scott has cross-referenced the page number of his journal entry for Tuesday, September 12.

36. "(A name for) an actor, usually one of outstanding ability, success, or fame. Now chiefly hist., with reference to David Garrick (1717–1779)," s.v. "Roscius."

37. "A Canadian; spec. a French Canadian," s.v. "Canuck."

38. "One of the race of original French colonists, chiefly small farmers or yeomen," s.v. "habitant."

39. From the start, Scott consecutively numbered the pages of his journal. Here he refers to pages 82 and 83 for his entry dated Wednesday, September 27.

40. Slang term for "an Irish person," s.v. "Pat."

41. "Alone, by oneself," s.v. "solus."

42. In 1826, a Patrick Buckley is listed as a physician in the district of Montreal. See *Quebec Almanack, 1826*, 78–79.

43. French phrase for nothing new.

44. In 1826, a Colin Miller is listed as a Deputy Assistant Commissaries General. See *Quebec Almanack, 1826*, 207–208.

45. This was probably the steamboat *Montreal*, constructed in 1819 to operate as a ferry between Laprairie and Montreal. See Frank Mackey, *Steamboat Connections: Montreal to Upper Canada, 1816–1843* (Montreal: McGill-Queen's University Press, 2000), 8.

46. In an 1820 directory for Montreal, a Patrick Savage, "joiner and cabinet-maker," is listed as residing at 83 Saint Paul Street. See Thomas Doige, *An Alphabetical List of the Merchants, Traders, and Housekeepers, Residing in Montreal*, 2nd ed. (Montreal: James Lane, 1820), 129, HathiTrust Digital Library at: https://

babel.hathitrust.org/cgi/pt?id=aeu.ark:/13960/t13n2xg0r;view=1up;seq=137 (original from University of Alberta), PDF (hereafter cited as Doige, *Alphabetical List of the Merchants*).

47. Mrs. Goodman has not been identified, nor has Miss Jane B.

48. The French phrase that Scott interjects here can be translated as "truly a beautiful little girl." My thanks to independent scholar Margaret Lynch-Brennan for her assistance in translating this phrase.

49. Samuel W. H. Leslie is listed as a doctor in the city of Quebec. See *Quebec Almanack, 1826*, 78. According to Jack Verney's biography of Edmund Bailey O'Callaghan, Dr. Leslie would become a colleague of Scott's friend O'Callaghan. After the latter moved to Quebec in 1828, both he and Dr. Leslie served as physicians working at the Emigrants' Hospital in Quebec during 1828–1829. Since Scott identifies Dr. Leslie in this entry as an acquaintance of his, it is quite possible that Leslie was the one who first introduced Scott to O'Callaghan. See Verney, *O'Callaghan*, page 232, footnote 22.

50. Mr. Usher has not been identified.

51. Rositer Hoyle was clerk to the Superintendent General of the Office of the Indian Department. He resided at 10 St. Phillippe Street. This was possibly the family who Scott visits. See Doige, *Alphabetical List of the Merchants*, 32, 85.

52. Scott actually booked passage on the *New Swiftsure*, a steamboat running between Montreal to Quebec and owned by John Molson and Sons. Scott's name appears on its passenger list for November 17, 1826. See Molson Coors Canada; Toronto, Ontario, Canada; St. Lawrence Steamboat Company Papers 1812–1892, MSS 475, vol. 29, *New Swiftsure* (April 25–November 21, 1826—Passengers, Freight and Fuel), accessed August 30, 2016, through Ancestry.com. The original is in the Rare Books and Special Collections, McGill University Library, Montreal, Quebec (hereafter cited as St. Lawrence Steamboat Company Papers).

53. Mr. Fry has not been identified.

54. The records for the steamboat company show that there were five first-class passengers onboard when the *New Swiftsure* departed Montreal, but only three were traveling all the way to Quebec. Additionally, there were forty-five steerage passengers, of whom twenty-one were traveling all the way to Quebec. Remaining passengers disembarked at scheduled stops in William Henry (Sorel) and Trois-Rivières (Three Rivers). See St. Lawrence Steamboat Company Papers.

55. Dr. Anthony Von Iffland, "physician, surgeon and epidemiologist" (1798–1876). Refer to the *Dictionary of Canadian Biography* online at: http://www.biographi.ca/en/bio/iffland_anthony_von_10E.html for a full biography of Von Iffland, accessed May 14, 2018. In his bibliography of O'Callaghan, Jack Verney records that during the Asian Cholera outbreak of 1832 in Quebec, doctors Iffland and O'Callaghan were appointed medical directors of the new Cholera Hospital established to deal with the medical crisis. See Verney, *O'Callaghan*, 53.

56. A Thomas Fortier is listed as a doctor in the "District des Trois-Rivieres." This may be the person Scott called on. See *Quebec Almanack, 1826,* 80.

57. Batiscan is located on the north side of the St. Lawrence River, above Three Rivers.

58. "Of attributes: resembling what pertains to the seraphim; worthy of a seraph; ecstatically adoring," s.v. "seraphic." From the context of Scott's sentence, I believe he means that the resulting music was not always heavenly.

59. In September 1825, Bernhard, the Duke of Saxe-Weimar Eisenach, making the journey from Quebec to Montreal aboard the St. Lawrence Steamboat Company's *Lady Sherbrook* (a sister ship to the *Swiftsure*), provides a vivid description of the "continual devouring":

> In this boat they have four meals daily, and at every repast they drove me from my writing place. In the morning at seven o'clock, they ring the bell for the passengers to rise and dress; at eight o'clock breakfast is served, which consists of tea, coffee, sausages, ham, beefsteak, and eggs; at twelve, they take luncheon; at four dine; at eight, take tea; and an hour before every meal they set the table.

See Bernhard, *Travels,* 96.

60. Lac-Saint-Pierre is above Montreal where the St. Lawrence River widens out to form a lake at the south end of which, just above Sorel, are many islands.

61. Scott has misspelled Beloeil. The community of Beloeil seems to have been interchangeably used with the mountain rising just beyond it: Mont Saint Hilaire. See Pierre Louis Lapointe, "Beloeil," last edited March 4, 2015, *The Canadian Encyclopedia* at: http://www.thecanadianencyclopedia.ca/en/article/beloeil/, accessed October 7, 2016.

62. "Phrases (many proverbial) expressing love or affection for one's own home, home country, etc.," s.v. "home sweet home." The song "Home Sweet Home," was written by John Howard Payne for his 1823 play *The Maid of Milan.* See "John Howard Payne Papers, 1813–1825," RBM 2852, Biographical or Historical Note, Penn State University Libraries at: https://www.libraries.psu.edu/findingaids/2852.htm, accessed October 7, 2016.

Afterword

1. *Montreal Almanack,* 21. There were no law schools or formal university training in Quebec prior to the 1840s. Legal education was based on a clerkship or apprenticeship with a commissioned lawyer. Such apprenticeships typically lasted five years. See Jean-Philippe Garneau, "The Lawyers, The Courtroom and The Pub-

lic Sphere: Defending the French Law Tradition in British Quebec at the Turn of the Nineteenth Century," *Quademi Storici,* Nouva Serie, 47.141 (3) (2012): 804.

2. Biographical information on Vallières is found at: James H. Lambert in collaboration with Jacques Monet, "Vallières de Saint-Réal, Joseph-Rémi," in *Dictionary of Canadian Biography,* vol. 7, University of Toronto/Université Laval, 2003– , http://www.biographi.ca/en/bio/vallieres_de_saint_real_joseph_remi_7E.html, accessed May 15, 2018 (hereafter cited as Lambert, "Vallières").The Scott partnership with Vallières is specifically mentioned in this entry, as well as the authors' assessment of its modest success.

3. Lambert, "Vallières." In the entry for "Parti canadien," in *The Canadian Encyclopedia,* Maxime Dagenais offers this brief overview:

> In 1826, members of the Parti canadien began calling themselves the Parti patriote. They were no longer fighting for a stronger assembly, but for the rights and existence of an entire nation. By adopting the title of patriote, they linked their party with other national-democratic movements of the period, such as the American and French Revolutions. In the 1830s, the party continued to use its powers over taxation to increase the Legislative Assembly's authority in colonial government—first leading to a political stalemate and then to rebellion.

See Maxime Dagenais, "Parti canadien," last edited February 18, 2016, *The Canadian Encyclopedia,* http://www.thecanadianencyclopedia.ca/en/article/parti-canadien/, accessed May 18, 2018. The complexities of Canadian politics are far outside the scope of this edited transcription of Scott's travel journal. While he certainly would have had to navigate those complexities during his subsequent legal career, only the barest fragments are presently known about that career.

4. Donald Fyson, *Magistrates, Police, and People: Everyday Criminal Justice in Quebec and Lower Canada, 1764–1837* (Toronto: Published for The Osgoode Society for Canadian Legal History by the University of Toronto Press, 2006), 127. Fyson articulates the role of a clerk of the peace: "Justices of the peace in England and the colonies often relied heavily on their clerks for legal advice. Their main assistant was usually the clerk of the peace, generally a paid professional whose main responsibilities were to create and manage the records of the justices' courts and organize the courts themselves" (125).

5. *Appendix, No. 2, to the Fourth Volume of the Journals of the Legislative Assembly of the Province of Canada, from the 28th day of November, 1844, to the 29th day of March, 1846* [. . .] (Montreal: Rollo Campbell, 1845), Appendix BBB, Return of the Names, &c. of the persons who have been appointed to any Office of Emolument in Lower Canada, from the 10th February, 1841, to the 9th December, 1843; prepared in pursuance of an Address of the Legislative Assembly, dated 4th December, 1844, no page number, HathiTrust Digital Library at: https://babel.

hathitrust.org/cgi/pt?id=chi.74612090;view=1up;seq=9 (original from University of Chicago), PDF. At the time, the Court of Appeals at Quebec could hear appeals from any court in Canada, except from the Admiralty Court. Its members included the "Governor, or Lieutenant-Governor, the members of the Executive Council, the Chief Justice of the Province, and the Chief Justice of Montreal; . . ." See Charles Clark, *A Summary of Colonial Law, the Practice of the Court of Appeals from the Plantations, and of the Laws and Their Administration in All the Colonies; with the Charters of Justice, Orders in Council, &c. &c. &c.* (London: S. Sweet, 1834), 401–402, HathiTrust Digital Library at: https://babel.hathitrust.org/cgi/pt?id=aeu.ark:/13960/t21c3340m;view=1up;seq=430 (original from University of Alberta), PDF.

    6. "Report of the Select Committee Appointed to Inquire into the State of the Judicial and Parliamentary Records in Lower Canada," *Appendix, No. 3, to the Fifth Volume of the Journals of the Legislative Assembly of the Province of Canada* [. . .] (Montreal: Rollo Campbell, 1846), Appendix KK, May 19, 1846, no page numbers, HathiTrust Digital Library at: https://babel.hathitrust.org/cgi/pt?id=chi.74687000;view=1up;seq=200;size=125 (original from University of Chicago), PDF.

    7. There were two rebellions against the British government, one in Lower Canada led by Louis-Joseph Papineau and the Patriotes Party, in which Scott's friend Edmund O'Callaghan was a prominent member, and a smaller one in Upper Canada led by William Mackenzie. Both revolts grew from long-simmering resentments—particularly by French Canadians in Lower Canada—against arbitrary British colonial policies that the British administration in London consistently refused to reform. In November 1837 violence broke out in Lower Canada "in a series of skirmishes and battles between Patriote rebels and trained British regulars as well as anglophone volunteers." The rebels were decisively beaten and their leaders, including O'Callaghan, fled to the United States, where they continued to attempt to support the Patriote cause, including launching a second armed incursion into Canada aided by American volunteers. Poorly organized, this action failed, effectively ending the Patriote cause but also eventually leading to British colonial government reform and the union of Lower and Upper Canada into the province of Canada in 1841. For a fuller summary of both rebellions, see Phillip A. Buckner, "Rebellions of 1837–38," revised by Richard Foot, last edited November 4, 2016, *The Canadian Encyclopedia, Historica Canada*, 1985– , http://www.thecanadianencyclopedia.ca/en/article/rebellions-of-1837/, accessed April 26, 2017.

    8. "Alexander Stewart Scott," marriage record, Saint Andrew's Presbyterian Church, December 13, 1830, Quebec, Canada, Vital and Church Records (Drouin Collection), 1621–1968, accessed through Ancestry.com on November 15, 2016. Original is in the Gabriel Drouin, comp., *Drouin Collection*, Montreal, Quebec, Canada: Institut généalogique Drouin. His marriage was also published in the Tuesday, December 14 edition of *the Quebec Mercury*: "Married. On Monday the 13th inst. by the Revd. D. Harkness, Alexander Steward Scott, Esq. of this city, Advocate, to Miss Catherine, youngest daughter of the late Lieut. Colonel Charles

Fremont of Montreal." See "Married," *Quebec Mercury*, December 14, 1830, Biblio-thèque et Archives nationales du Québec at: http://numerique.banq.qc.ca/patrimoine/details/52327/1877421?docref=v5-9bLPLs5YeQURjluaT2g, accessed May 15, 2018.

9. For information of Catherine Susan Fremont's family, see: Pierre-Georges Roy, *La Famille Fremont* (Levis: n.p., 1902), 9, HathiTrust Digital Library at: https://babel.hathitrust.org/cgi/pt?id=mdp.39015025958029;view=1up;seq=17 (original from University of Michigan), PDF. For Charles-Jacques Frémont, see: Charles-Marie Bois-sonnault, "FRÉMONT, CHARLES-JACQUES," in *Dictionary of Canadian Biography*, vol. 9, University of Toronto / Université Laval, 2003– , http://www.biographi.ca/en/bio/fremont_charles_jacques_9E.html, accessed May 15, 2018.

10. "Jane Charlotte Catherine Stewart Scott, Baptême, 1831, Notre-Dame, Quebec, Quebec," Quebec, Canada, Vital and Church Records (*Drouin Collection*), 1621–1968, accessed through Ancestry.com on November 15, 2016. Original is in the Gabriel Drouin, comp., *Drouin Collection*, Montreal, Quebec, Canada: Institut généalogique Drouin. Only the year of Jane's baptism is apparently recorded; no month or day was identified.

11. Individual member family trees for Alexander Stewart Scott were identi-fied by the editor during searches of the website Ancestry.com undertaken in 2016.

12. "Alexander Stewart Scott, Enterrement, May 24, 1859, Saint Patrick, Quebec, Quebec," Quebec, Canada, Vital and Church Records (*Drouin Collection*), 1621–1968, accessed through Ancestry.com on November 15, 2016. Original is in the Gabriel Drouin, comp., *Drouin Collection*, Montreal, Quebec, Canada: Institut généalogique Drouin.

13. For information on Harrison and the quotation from the Toronto critic, see Carol Lowrey, "HARRISON, MARK ROBERT," in *Dictionary of Canadian Biography*, vol. 12, University of Toronto / Université Laval, 2003– , http://www.biographi.ca/en/bio/harrison_mark_robert_12E.html, accessed November 16, 2016.

14. J. M. Le Moine, *Quebec Past and Present: A History of Quebec, 1608–1876* (Quebec: Augustin Côté & Co., 1876), 286, HathiTrust Digital Library at: https://babel.hathitrust.org/cgi/pt?id=hvd.32044081320590;view=1up;seq=318 (original from Harvard University), PDF (hereafter cited as Le Moine, *Quebec Past and Present*).

15. Le Moine, *Quebec Past and Present*, 289–290.

Appendix One

1. Mr. Kenyon has not been identified.

2. An Elisha Sheldon is listed as a member of the Franklin County Medi-cal Society, which was founded in 1814. It is possible that this is the person Scott met at some point on his journey, although Scott does not enter Dr. Sheldon's first name, so we cannot be certain. See Lewis Cass Aldrich, ed., *History of Franklin and Grand Isle Counties, Vermont with Illustrations and Biographical Sketches of Some of*

the Prominent Men and Pioneers (Syracuse: D. Mason & Co., 1891), 262, Internet Archive at: https://archive.org/details/cu31924028837544/page/n283 (original from Cornell University Library), PDF.

3. The Barlow family was prominent in early nineteenth-century Fairfield, Vermont. Just which of the family members Scott met is impossible to determine without a first name. Fairfield is in Franklin County, and in November 1817 a Darius Sherman Barlow was admitted to that county's legal bar. In September 1825, Ebenezer Barlow joined the bar and the next year became a Register of Probate. Given Scott's interest in meeting and discussing the law, he may have met either of these members of the Barlow family. See Abby Maria Hemenway, ed., *The Vermont Historical Gazetteer: A Magazine Embracing a History of Each Town, Civil, Ecclesiastical, Biographical and Military*, vol. 2 (Burlington: A. M. Hemenway, 1871), 93–95, Internet Archive at: https://archive.org/details/vermonthistoric00winggoog/page/n110 (original Google Books), PDF.

Index

Note: Page numbers in *italics* indicate illustrations.

Spafford, Horatio Gates, 17, 143n1;
on Clifton Springs, 146nn32–33; on
Erie Canal, 152n7; on Manchester
Village, 146n31; on New York State
Capitol, 158nn5–7; on Palmyra,
143n1; on Vienna (NY), 145n28
Spencer, Benjamin T., 130n11
St. Albans (VT), 103
St. John's (now Saint-Jean-sur-
Richelieu), 35, 96, 98–101, *102*,
138n15; garrison at, 38, 101, *102*,
107, 138n19, 167n14; inhabitants
of, 111; maps of, *37*, *100*;
Revolutionary War battle at, 106,
108, 168n26; stagecoach route at,
37, 38, 111; steamboat service from,
39
St. John's Hotel (Palmyra), 8
St. Lawrence River steamboats, 35,
37, 115–117, 135n1, 137n13,
170nn52–54, 171n59
stagecoaches, *53*; to Albany, 86, *88*;
fares of, 124–127; to Laprairie, 111;
to Saratoga Springs, 13–14, 43, *44*;
to St. John's, *37*, 38; to Troy, 89; to
Whitehall, 92, *95*
steamboats, 12–13, 132n41; fares
of, 124–127, 164n10; on Hudson
River, 87; on Lake Champlain, 13,
40, *41*, 139n20, 164n10; on Lake
George, 13, 14, 139nn27–28; on St.
Lawrence River, 35, *37*, 115–116,
135n1, 137n13, 170nn52–54,
171n59
Steele & Son's Bookstore (Albany), 6–7
Stocking, Jeremiah, 57
Stockton, Benjamin B., 144n12
Stone, William L., 17
Sulphur Springs (NY), 61,
146nn32–33
Supreme Court of Judicature (NY),
142n6

Syracuse, *52*, *84*, 85–86

Talman, James J., 19
Taylor, Alan, 18–19
Tenney, Jonathan, 157n14
theater, 8–9, 108, 169n36; in
Montreal, 8, 36, 106, 131n24;
in Palmyra, 8, 56–57, 143n3; in
Quebec City, 119
Three Rivers (Trois Rivières, Quebec),
35, 115, 136n2
Ticonderoga (NY), 13, 39–42, *41*, 96,
139n27
travel journal genre, 21–23
Troy (NY), *47*, *88*, 89–92

Union College (Schenectady), 49,
140n1
United States Hotel (Saratoga Springs),
43
Utica, 49–52, *52*, *84*; Bagg's history
of, 141n3; Erie Canal at, *51*;
Lafayette's visit to, 141n5

Vallières de Saint-Réal, Joseph-Rémi,
117
Van Buren, Martin, 159n9
Van Schoonhoven, Geurt, 93, 96, 122,
161n1, 164n11
Verplanck, Johnston, *51*, *70*
Vienna (NY), 61, 145n28
Von Iffland, Anthony, 115, 170n55

Wall, William Guy, *45*
Wallace, Elisha, 86, 121, 156n8
Walsh, Janet (Jean), 155n19
War of 1812, 3, 11, 151n3, 164n14;
aftermath of, 18–20, 138n19;
conclusion of, 15, 139n25
Waterloo, Battle of (1815), 19
Watervliet (NY) arsenal, *47*, 89,
159nn10–11

Made in the USA
Columbia, SC
23 January 2022